ODDS & ENDS*

BITS & PIECES

A memorable slice of life

By

Joye O'Keefe

Fireside

PUBLICATIONS
www.FiresidePubs.com

Fireside Publications
5144 Harbour Drive
Oxford, Florida 34484
www.firesidepubs.com

This book of essays and stories is a non-fiction work (although some
short stories written by the author are fiction) based on the true
experiences of the author as she experienced life over the past six
decades. Needless to say, her experiences and the eye through which she
saw life will be quite different from that of many of her readers. Please
keep an open mind and view a different "Slice of Life" from what you
may have seen before.

To order additional copies, please visit:
http://.firesidepubs.com   or
Contact the author at:
joyeeliz828@aol.com

FORWARD

How best can a human life be described? This is an interesting question requiring a complex answer. Most lives ride a wave of joyous experiences through the many births, weddings and personal accomplishments of friends and family. Additional journeys are made into valleys of deep heartbreak where others' loses affect all who suffer misfortune around them. The rest of their lives are then colored by the many shades of emotion that lie in between.

Words such as smiles, happiness, laughter, contentment or moments of peace and comfort help to put these feelings into verbal context and lighter fare. Far more serious are the other times reflected by words like sadness, regret, anger, frustration, indecision, worry and pain.

A multitude of words each replacing another in a different instance scramble to describe the moments of time in which we live. Certain circumstances and feelings soon fade away while others may stay with us for the remainder of our lives.

The following stories and poems, some true, others drawn from the depths of imagination, have one common element: they all in their own irreplaceable way describe a slice of the odds and ends or bits and pieces of life.

DEDICATION

This book of snippets taken from treasured moments of my life is dedicated to Mom and Dad and to all the other relatives and friends who mean so much to me. You are all precious to me because you make life worth living. You know who you are, as do I.

ACKNOWLEDGEMENTS

I owe so very much to Grandma Whitmore who unknowingly helped me to see poetry in a new personal light. And to my son Erik, who as a teenager, entertained me with his original spooky stories. "The Bowler" found near the end of this collection is a product of his active imagination.

My heartfelt thanks go to my daughters, Nikki Shell for her technical support for this book, and DeeDee Casagrande for her assistance with so many things over the years. I especially want to thank both of them for their unfailing faith and patience.

Diane Banks lent her creative eye to select the pictures so suitably introducing each section; then she relentlessly typed the pages of the manuscript. I owe you so much, Diane. Thank you.

Thanks to Stephanie and Chris for the use of their "hands." May you also have 50 Years of Love.

Last, but not to be forgotten, my editor, Lois Bennett who gave me guidance, counsel, and her expertise which truly made this all possible.

CATS

AND

DOGS

CATS AND DOGS

Are you a dog lover? Or a cat lover, perhaps? Or do your affections reach out to all-things-animal?

Perchance, the poems and short story in this section will please everyone who has ever had, does have, or will have, at some time in their unpredictable future a beloved four-legged furry or hairy pet.

Enjoy!

Little Ugly

"FREE KITTENS," the sign said.

"Oh!" exclaimed Mark. "Let's stop and see the kittens. Can we have one?"

"Yeah, Mom, please?" Beth echoed.

"We'll stop and look, but I'm not sure we're ready for another cat right now," their mom said. Thoughts of Sammy, their beloved cat who had died of old age just one week ago, ran through her mind.

Six playful kittens scampered around teasing one another with colorful yarn and tiny toys. Two were calico with colorful markings. Two others were black and white, with mask-like spots covering their eyes. Another beautiful kitty, its soft body covered in long gray fur, purred quietly as it looked up at them. The last kitten, however, hardly received a glance from the children. His fur was medium length and silky, but he was black with splotches of gray and tan all mixed together. It looked as though he'd been splattered with all the colors and then a hand had smeared them into an unsightly mess. No white outline or spots were there to alleviate his dark, dismal coloring.

The kids fell in love with the gray one. Even Mom could not resist him. So, "Smokey" became the first kitten to find a home.

As the days passed, one by one each of the kittens found a home. That is, all the kittens except Little Ugly found homes.

When folks came to look, Little Ugly would run up to them to get their attention then rub against their legs and purr loudly. But, no one wanted him. He was very unhappy when all his brothers and sisters had left. Several people stopped by to see him, but no one wanted to take him home. As each day and then a week passed, he became more and more lonely.

One day a car pulled into the driveway, but the sad little kitten hid his head, knowing it would not be anyone for him to love. He continued to lie in the sun and pretended to be asleep.

"Just one left," said the owner. "Not much to look at, but a nice cat nevertheless."

Little Ugly murmured sadly, as hands tightened around his body and he was carefully lifted into the arms of a little girl.

"Oh how sweet! What a lovely soft kitten," she crooned, as she petted him gently and held him close to her chest.

Little Ugly could not believe his ears! She didn't seem to find him ugly. He started to purr and snuggled in her arms.

"Can I keep him, Daddy? Please! He's just perfect."

"Of course, Anne," her dad answered. "That's why we came here, to find you a kitten to keep you company.

"Thank you, Daddy. I'm going to call him 'Handsome Hairy' and just 'Handsome' for short. I'll take very good care of him, I promise." She smiled and her blue eyes seemed to sparkle. She walked slowly back toward the car while Handsome Hairy's former owner shook his head, perplexed.

"You're certainly welcome to the kitten, but he's just not a beautiful cat. Never will be."

"That's because you only see what's on the outside," Anne's dad said. "Anne sees the heart and the goodness within.

The man stood there with a questioning look on his face.

"She may not see everything that other people catch sight of, but she can feel the love and warmth coming from the heart."

Anne's dad smiled, gently.

"You see, my daughter is blind."

Old Folks Shouldn't Have Puppies

In "dog years," Fred was nearing about 105 when he died.
The old couple, both in their 80s, missed him. They cried.
One day to his still-grieving wife, the old man tearfully said,
"We need to get another dog, Dear; just like our gentle Fred.

An adorable miniature dog, purebred too, wasn't hard to find.
He cost a pretty penny, but the ageing couple didn't mind.
This pristine ball of bouncy white fluff, made their hearts sing.
Little did they know just how much complexity it would bring.

On the first night home, the pup whined then wept and cried.
Tossing, turning, and missing sleep, the old couple just sighed.
"Maybe we'll let him sleep in our bed, but only for tonight.
He'll soon get used to us; then I'm sure he will be all right."

Little Fluffy yapped happily, judging the arrangement to be fine.
Soon he slept there every night and hardly ever would he whine.
Distressingly, they couldn't remember the new puppy's name.
So, it became much easier to call him and the old dog the same.

At first, they were ever so proud, walking their dog so adorable.
He liked to run and play. "Not us," said they, feeling deplorable.
Pulled at the leash, circled round them and barked, then he'd race
Until their arms grew tired; they needed to walk at a leisurely pace.

Bending over to pick up his deposit, or his doggie dish for food,
Kept getting harder; still they loved him, he elevated their mood.
He developed terrible habits neither of them had energy to break.
While they sat, he'd jump, scratching, bouncing till legs did ache.

By stretching, into pockets he'd sneak – pants, jacket or sweater.
To pull, chew up, run with stuff, even cash – Kleenex was better.
Leading them on a merry chase, fun was in winning – not defeat.
Soon they coached him to relinquish his prize for a yummy treat.

So whenever he wanted a treat, just guess what that stinker'd do.
Of course! He'd run with whatever he found, even if a dirty shoe.
Sadly they covered their beautiful white couch with a linen sheet,
Because he'd jump up there and bark at anyone walking on the street.

First a baby, then a toddler, soon pup became an unruly teenager.
"Yes, he'll settle down." The old man said, "I'll make a wager."
But shortly, the old man became ill and soon he left this life.
Leaving the wild child in the sole care of his frail elderly wife.

She tried to humor him and walk him, but he pulled her too hard.
She fell, in the street of all places, missing the softness of the yard.
Neighbors helped, and fortunately she hadn't even a broken bone.
But it was plain for all who saw, she could no longer remain alone.

The children were called; someone would come in a month or two.
Then one day a neighbor found her very ill. What were they to do?
Caring neighbors offered help until an ambulance carted her away.
Then her missing children rushed to assist her that very next day.

Happily unaware, the pup was left to stay at a neighbor's home.
Finally, her children realized she could no longer be on her own.
What will happen to her? Should she live with a child out of state?
The adored wild pup will likely outlive her. What is to be his fate?

Yes, old folks need a cuddly companion. We do understand that.
But maybe something sweet, comfy, like an adorable purring cat.
Can't hardly pet or cuddle birds, lizards, or out of style guppies.
Old dogs are okay, but it is a fact:
Old Folks Shouldn't Have Puppies.

MO

We have a white cat; he's a sight to behold.
For years and years I've always been told,
Pure white cats in all cases have deaf ears.
But I know for a fact, mine definitely hears.

Because when born, perhaps, he wasn't pure white,
A shock of gray streaked his head – an adorable sight!
Looked very much like a Mohawk-type cut of hair.
Or a smudge of soot, or lump of coal situated there.

Sometimes he's called Smudge, but really named MO.
Everyone, even the kids next door, loved him so.
We also had an old gray cat; Smokey was his name.
Not very original, but it portrayed him just the same.

Now Smokey got too cantankerous to eat his food dry,
So, soft, tasty, canned food we decided to let him try.
It usually worked very well for our poor, elderly cat.
Of course, there was MO; he had to have a taste of that.

After Smokey left this world, MO still fancied his treat.
A quarter of a can at a time, that's all I'd let him eat.
But alas and alack! At Christmas-time one snowy year,
I slipped away from home to visit my children, so dear.

For Christmas, Norm considered offering him a treat.
Instead of a quarter can, he granted a whole one to eat.
Little did he know what a monster, he now had created.
Just a small amount would no longer make MO elated.

Every day thereafter, Mo's behavior became very bad.
He's wise enough to know there's more food to be had.
He wants it morning, noon, night and then in between.
My Mo has gotten to be the orneriest cat I've ever seen.

I have to firmly say "NO!" and draw an inflexible line.
Or that feline would be gorging on soft food all the time.
If heard then by my neighbors, they'd get quite a shock.
Wondering what happened to that nice lady on the block?

At best, it's just that I'm politically incorrect in my speech.
At worst, that I'm prejudiced, not practicing what I preach.
Because each day he yowls and mews, running to and fro,
I can be heard exclaiming, "No MO!"
                         "No! MO!"
                              "NO! MO!"

Little Girl Lost

One sunny day she played with her dog in the yard.
She opened the gate, finding it was not all that hard.

Just took a walk to see everything that she might see.
She could never know what trouble would come to be.

Discovered missing, her parents sounded the alarm.
Frantic, they pleaded, "Please keep her from harm."

The child now lost, could not find her way back home.
But the dog stayed right beside her, so she wasn't alone.

The search went on unsuccessfully until it was night.
More prayers went up, "Please let her be all right."

It turned cold; she was frightened where they were huddled.
The dog gave her warmth; she fell asleep as they cuddled.

Morning came. The dog could be seen from the helicopter ride.
The child they could not see – might she be there by his side?

Yes! She had been protected while holding the dog tight.
She's alive – rescued – and with just a touch of frost-bite.

The protective love of the dog kept her safe and eased her fear.
To her family, that dog will always be extra especially dear.

For he's a hero – stayed by her side 'til she could be found.
Yes! A real miracle it is. She's now home, safe and sound.

LIFE

Life

In the English language, the word "life" has a multitude of connotations, which mean many things to different people.

The "good life," to some individuals, means being rich and famous. To others, it encompasses no more than having a home, a job, and people who love them.

Most of us would agree that a thief who steals possessions or money is living a "bad life." To the thief, perhaps he thinks he is living the good life – at least until he's caught.

A "wasted life," many would agree, might be someone whose abuse of drugs or alcohol has prevented them from reaching their full potential. To that person, life may be perceived as being comfortable or "safe."

Perhaps, a son who refuses to go into the family business, but instead travels the world, by his family's standard is considered as having an "empty" or "wasted life." The son, however, sees his life as fulfilled, educational, happy, because he sees more of the world than most people see, learns new skills and develops a multitude of friends.

Who is right? There is no absolute answer as the minor depictions of life may relate little to the world at large.

We must not forget the importance of "Life's Lessons." They are innumerable but all are important in different areas of living. Not the least of these lessons to be learned is…

- Treat everyone you meet with kindness. If that is not possible, be decent. You never know when they may re-enter your life or what role they might play, sometime in the future.
- Along with the large, life changing events that occur, our existence contains all the odds and ends of our being alive.

17

SAVE A LIFE

Joe sauntered into the living room with his mind totally focused on tomorrow's basketball game. He winced as his mom suddenly broke into his daydream.

"Oh, good Joe, you're just in time to see this. It's important," she called out.

"See what?" Joe grumbled, not willing to move his mind away from the visions of a cheering crowd as he became a hero making those three point baskets, to something mundane on television.

"They are giving a demonstration on the Heimlich maneuver," his mom explained"

"Heimlich maneuver?" The name rang a bell in Joe's mind. "Oh, like when a person is choking?"

"Exactly right" his mom said, pleased that he understood. Maybe there was hope for this boy after all. "Some boy saved his teacher's life the other day," she continued. "He used it when she was choking on a cough drop."

"Do I HAVE to watch it? I'm just working on some basketball moves here."

Joe," his mom admonished, "Just because no one chokes on a basketball, doesn't mean it can never happen around you. Everyone should know what to do. It could be the most important thing a person can learn."

"I thought you just gave them a good whack on the back," Joe said as he reluctantly sat down. After a short version of the student's heroics, Joe heard, "No longer do we treat conscious adult choking victims with a whack on the back between the shoulder blades as we used to. We've learned that it often lodges the obstruction further. One exception is a baby. We'll discuss that tomorrow."

18

"Well, that answers that concern, doesn't it?" his mom observed.

Joe watched, half listening, with his thoughts on the moves he planned to make to lead his team to victory. The basketball game was just too important to put out of his mind completely.

Demonstrating on a person standing quietly in front of him, the instructor continued.

"You stand behind the victim, make a fist, reach around and press the fist, thumb first, into the victims upper abdomen, below the rib cage, but above the belly button. Cover the fist with your other hand. Pull the fist sharply in and upwards – much like you are hugging the person. This pushes on the diaphragm and will expel the object.

"Sounds simple enough, doesn't it Joe?" his mom asked. "Here, let's try it on each other."

"I see how to do it. It's not necessary to try it too." Joe felt embarrassed that his mom actually expected him to put his arms around her waist.

Mom, however, insisted that he practice.

With a little adjustment, Joe found the correct place to put his fist, but he certainly didn't pull up very hard.

"I think you've got the idea," she said, "but if someone was really choking, you'd have to do it harder, Joe."

"But what if that person is very large?" Joe asked. "Like Mr. Statson. Not too many people can get their arms around him."

"Weren't you listening?" Joe's mom looked at him suspiciously. "They mentioned that. It's possible to have a person lie on his back. You must straddle his legs and push up on the diaphragm from that position."

"Oh," said Joe, abashed he had missed that part. "Well, I'll probably never need to know that stuff anyway."

Saturday morning before Joe was completely awake, his mom came into his room. "I have to leave for work early. Blaine is coming over to play with Lizzei after lunch. "I'm sorry but, I need you to watch them until Dad gets home."

"Aw, Mom! I was going to Tim's and shoot some baskets." Joe hadn't made a single three pointer during the game last night, in spite of his daydreams.

"You can go after Dad gets home. You know Lizzie's too young to be left alone," his mom said sternly.

Joe sighed. He did love six year old Lizzie, but babysitting wasn't his favorite thing to do, especially on a Saturday with that basketball hoop calling his name.

The afternoon passed slowly. Lizzie and Blaine were playing and chattering noisily. They occasionally snitched a piece of candy from under Joe's nose, laughing joyfully as he pretended to try to catch them.

Suddenly there was silence and Blaine cried, "Joe! Joe! Come quick! Something's wrong with Lizzie!"

Startled, Joe jumped up and ran to the playroom. Lizzie stood in the middle of the floor. Her face was red, her eyes bulging as she waved her hands helplessly in the air. Joe felt paralyzed.

"What happened?" he yelled.

Blaine started crying, "I just gave her a piece of candy and she started acting funny," he sobbed!

Joe knew! The candy was stuck in Lizzie's throat! He ran to her, to hit her on the back, but suddenly the warning from Thursday night's program rang loud in his ears.

"DO NOT WHACK ON THE BACK!"

As Lizzie's face turned from red to pale and bluish, his mind screamed, Heimlich Maneuver!

He wrapped his arms around his sister, made the fist, put it in place and pulled up. Nothing happened. Frantic, he pulled harder. Once! Twice! Suddenly, with a gagging sound, out flew the peppermint candy and a gob of yellow vomit! Joe gasped. *Yuk! They never said that would happen* was the thought that crossed his mind as he heard Lizzie draw in a ragged breath and start crying.

"Dear God, Thank you," he breathed as he turned his sister toward him and hugged her. "It's okay. You're fine now." He didn't even mind she smeared his shirt with the slime of her vomit.

As Joe cleaned up the mess, he explained to Blaine that Lizzie had choked on the candy and calling for help saved her life.

"It did?" Blaine asked as he and Lizzie looked at each other in surprise.

After Blaine had left, but before his dad got home, it started raining. Joe sat glumly on the couch, feeling sorry for himself. There'd be no basket shooting today.

Then Lizzie came in, hugged him and whispered in his ear, "Thank you, Joey, for saving my life."

As Joe hugged her to him, he suddenly didn't feel a bit bad about the missed basketball practice. After all, there was always tomorrow. And there would be tomorrow for Lizzie too.

LET ME FINISH MY...

A group of young teen girls at camp were sitting around, getting to know each other. Now it's my turn.

"I was raised in Joliet, Illinois – because I was born in a prison..."

"What?" Someone yelled, interrupting me. "You were born in a prison?"

"What did your mother do?" another shouted.

"No, she didn't..."

"Did she steal something?"

"No, the only thing she ever stole was my Dad's heart. She..."

"I know! I bet she embezzled something. I just learned that word," another said proudly.

"No! No! She..."

Miss Know-It-All chimed in. "No goofy. Embezzled is another word for stealing. Only you get a lot more money."

"No guys, she..."

"Did she kill somebody?" another blurted out.

If looks could kill, I might have been found guilty right then.

"No! Of course not! She..."

"Did she beat the other kids and starve 'em? One obviously over-sensitive girl asked with her eyes leaking tears. "I've heard of people going to jail for that."

"No! She didn't do anything! I just..."

"What? She was imprisoned under false pretenses?" Miss Know-It-All questioned. I think her dad was a lawyer.

"No! She..."

"Well, then, why was she in prison?" they chorused.

"She wasn't! She..."

"Yeh, were you adopted from an evil mom and given to a nice one?"

"No! Will you let me finish a sentence here? I started…"

"Oh, weird! People finish a sentence in prison. How do you explain that?"

"Hey! Let me finish what I was going to say! I was raised in Joliet, Illinois – because I was born in a prison town!"

LIFE STEPS

At birth, there are none.

Then, along come Baby steps: wobbly, faltering, growing into...

Toddler steps: better balanced, faster, stronger, morphing into...

Childhood steps: running, jumping, skipping, occasional stumbling, climbing, bouncing, scuffing, twirling, until along comes...

Teen-age steps: long purposeful strides, urgent, happy skips, and quick bouncy half-steps or those that become slow and dragging giving a sense of depression. Dancing, some in rhythm, others not even close. Sport steps include running, jumping, sliding, kicking, bounding, while fan steps add stomping, quick-in-place steps, elevated on toes or in-place jumping. Then, as life matures, it settles into...

Adult steps: these comprehensive steps are inclusive of all those mentioned above and usually last much longer than any of the prior categories. Consider the slow rocking steps when comforting a baby; those hurried steps when used to finish a deadline or chores; steps sometimes slow and halting as they pace with a toddler, or a grandparent running to protect or play with a child; walking, jogging or running for exercise; ponderous for unwelcome chores or burdens of the heart; quick joyful to meet a friend or heading for entertainment; sad, slow, reluctant steps when saying good-bye to loved ones.

Finally, the last steps of life: slow, shuffling, painful, careful steps, uncertain yet determined or hesitant, faltering, becoming weaker, until...

The steps of life are no more.

Spoof on *LY* and *ING*

They say not to use too many words ending in *L Y* and *I N G*. But without them how weird our sentences would be.

The cat was happily running, jumping in the lushly flowering yard, chasing beautifully colored butterflies. OR
The cat was happy run and jump in the lush flower yard, chase beautiful butterflies.

Suddenly, hearing a growling sound, she paused. A frightening, snarling dog started chasing the sadly inadequately protected cat. OR
Sudden, hear a growl sound, she paused. A frighten, snarl dog started chase the sad inadequate protected cat.

He impatiently was waiting for the lovely, classmate who smiled so adoringly. OR
He impatient was wait for the love classmate who smiled so adore.

Suddenly, there she was, looking longingly around the room. OR
Sudden, there she was look long around the room.

As he was starting to rise, the teacher yelled loudly, "Everyone should be sitting quietly. OR
As he was start to rise, the teacher yelled loud, "Everyone should be sit quiet."

Sadly, he found himself humbly sitting down. A magnificently, marvelously, amazing opportunity lost. OR

Sad, he found himself humble sit down. A magnificent, marvelous amaze opportunity lost.

I love endings with *ly* and *ing*. But I know, not used carefully, might be tedious to tell and hard to show.

SNOWBIRD OVERVIEW

The term "snowbird" always brought to my northern mind, a chirpy, cute bird who loved to flutter and fly in the snow. But when my Las Vegas conditioned husband, with an invite from my dear sister, decided we'd try Florida for the winter months, I learned something new.

Snowbird is a dirty word.

The folks who brave the summer heat and humidity to live in Florida year around really are special. But, "You're a SNOWBIRD," they sneer as they grumble about crowds, traffic and long lines.

However, to fully understand, you must open your hearts and minds – not just your eyes. For snowbirds have a lot to give you, more than just headaches. And we may have great things to teach you.

For instance: We teach you patience. Long lines can give you time to reflect on your inner self – strengths, goal, hopes, dreams. Waiting quietly, slows your heart and keeps you from running here and there carelessly, frantic and troubled. Instead, you can glide through life in a peaceful "Zen" state.

We help you with driving. Do you have any idea how FAST you people go? Learned early, if approaching a light and it turns yellow, I'd better go through it because the guy behind me surely will. Not to mention you might learn some whole new hand signals and words.

We also teach you to use your time wisely when getting ready to go somewhere really early – keeps you from forgetting an important article of clothing, your money, or your spouse.

We are good for the digestion. If you don't want to stand in line, eat early. Not only do you get the Early Bird Special prices, but eating leisurely and early, assures you that your stomach will not be overloaded at bed time. You also have a lot more time during the long evening to relax and enjoy your friends –keeps the days from passing too quickly.

We are good for your health. With so many snowbirds taking up the doctor's time, you may not get an appointment for two months. That teaches you to take care of your health while you wait. Also you become adept in the art of first aid so you'll not waste time and gas running to the doctor for every little cut, bruise, sniffle, sneeze, cough and that ole headache. You could become close to earning a medical degree with all that you learn.

You get the enjoyment of giving us directions. After several months away, Snowbirds can be confused about the best way to get to a specific place. You all get SO much pleasure from telling us where to go.

We considerately give you all six to eight months of decreased traffic. Think how frustrated you'd be if we all lived here year around. Count your blessings!

Lastly, it's been asked, by Brett Burns, "If it's snowbird season, why can't we shoot them?" Well, game birds always have been shot and served on our tables. If you would shoot a snowbird, you'd have to change its name. Because it would look mighty peculiar perched on a platter, in the middle of your dinner table – naked as a JAYBIRD!

28

METABOLISM

Most people understand what metabolism is. Basically it's how your body uses and burns the calories you take in and converts it to energy for growing and renewing cells. There are high normal or low metabolism rates.

Unfortunately, my husband, Norm has the metabolism rate of a roaring train, while mine has the speed of a comatose sloth. Life is not fair.

For instance, he had to prep for a medical test – clear liquids for 24 hours and nothing to eat or drink for half a day until the test was completed. He dropped five pounds. I had the same test, except I was on clear liquids for 48 hours and nothing else 'til suppertime the day of the test. At that, I could only have soup and salad. I didn't expect great results but losing a couple of pounds would have been nice. I lost NOTHING! Nada, zip, zilch, zero. I HATE his metabolism!

He drinks highly sweetened tea. I drink unsweetened tea. When we occasionally drink pop, he drinks regular, I drink diet. We share a small pizza. He gains nothing. I gain at least two pounds. Rarely do we snack while watching TV, but when he does, he has popcorn, nuts or caramel corn. I get to cross stitch and keep my hands clean. I hate his metabolism!

I once told him, I don't eat chocolate every day, but sometimes I really need to have it.

"No problem," he kindly said and bought a package of Hershey's Miniatures. Yum, my favorite. About four days later, the urge hit. I ran to the cupboard and pulled out the package. IT WAS EMPTY!

He'd eaten ALL of them, and, never gained an ounce doing it. I would have gained at least five pounds. I hate his metabolism!

Sometimes I make chocolate pudding for dessert. He gets three nice bowls for after supper and before bed. I get to scrape the pan.

The worst thing is, if there's no pudding, he immediately has cookies and milk; then he has them again before he goes to bed. I rarely eat before bed but when I do, I get a handful of baby carrots and six prunes. I REALLY hate his metabolism.

Every evening, especially when the weather is cold, I can feel my metabolism sinking into hibernation mode. I get colder and colder until, by my bedtime, I feel frozen. Norm usually goes to bed before I do, so his side of the bed is really warm. Most times, he allows me to snuggle up to him until I warm up enough to sleep. Why, it's like having my very own flameless furnace under the covers.

Yeah, life still isn't fair, but sometimes,

I LOVE his metabolism!

CAVERNS

Missouri's National Treasure, in 2008 was 75 years old,
Its history and ancient beauties are amazing for all to behold.
Though Osage Indians always knew of this great, awesome thing,
In 1720, Philipp Renault went to see what exploration would bring.

Indians found streaks of glittering yellow in the walls of the cave.
Renault excitedly thought *GOLD!* To this, all his attention he gave.
That's how he discovered the largest cave west of Mississippi River.
But, sadly he learned, of the sought after gold the cave was not a giver.

The yellow metal, saltpeter it was, aka, Potassium Nitrate.
The nitrate was needed to make gunpowder. Was that not great?
One hundred forty-four years of mining followed discovery.
But many disputes for control of the cave came to be.

Existing through the Civil War, when the South in the year of 1864,
Destroyed a Union gunpowder stand, and mining was no more.
The locals of the 1890's came up with an idea that never was beat.
During summer months hold *"cave parties,"* to avoid the extreme heat.

The 50 x 50 foot room was called "The Ballroom," not by chance.
Because that was where so many people could cool off and dance.
Charles Ruepple bought the cave to continue the dances in 1898.
But that year's destiny was held in the strong hand of fate.

For that very year was the birth of Lester Benton Dill.
He loved caving; and in 1933 bought the cave for his own will.
He changed the caves' name and added the word "caverns" too.
Possibly, in his hearts' mind, was there something more he knew?

31

He offered tours to the public, but still continued to explore.
One day, feeling a breeze through a crevice, he found much more.
Another huge cave, known now as the "Upper Level" came to be.
In that space stood a most-prized possession, there for all to see.

"Stage Curtain," he called it, an impressive sight nearly 70 feet tall.
Cleverly, "Theatre Room" was born, an amazing view for all.
Eight years later in 1941, another find launched that area into fame.
Forever after, the amazing caverns were never to be the same.

A severe drought depleted water levels, even at the cavern floor.
A different cool breeze excitedly hinted of perhaps another door.
Voila! Found a cave with artifacts traceable to a most infamous man,
The spot Jesse James and his men did hide, when from the law they ran.

Dubbed Jesse James' Hideout, it brought more people to   gawk and see.
What do you think could now the name of these famous caverns be?
Earlier called Saltpeter Cave, of a new name, Les Dill was the giver.
A hint – he took its name from the nearby winding, gentle river.

MERAMEC CAVERNS

Politically Correct – Isn't

Freedom of speech, means
we can say what we feel,
But calling people names
does usually offend.
Has nothing to do with
Political Correctness.
It's just as hurtful to others,
as it's always been.

Politically Correct seems to be,
To do away with any
mention of God
Because it offends a few.
To 94% of Americans,
that's very odd.
It's okay to use foul language,
take the Lord's name in vain.
And to lie, cheat, steal
or even kill,
all for a little personal gain.

It suggests, taking God
out of the oath in court,
out of the "pledge."
They'd take away the
Ten Commandments,
push us to the edge.

Politically Correct means
taking Christ out of Christmas,
getting rid of the manger Scene.
Deny the "Reason for the Season"
else some get provoked.

But, it's okay to offend
the Christians
it does seem.
To celebrate Hanukah,
Kwanza, or another day,
I'm the first to say,
"That is their right."
The same is not granted
to Christians,
wishing to celebrate
that Holy Night.

Remember, this country
was founded on
a deep belief in God.
That belief has placed America
on very special sod.

Politically Correct to
Christians, means including
God's Commandments
in Government, Courts,
Hearts and Home.
Then we all will be
free to choose:

34

Merry Christmas;

Happy Kwanza;

Happy Hanukah;

And To all,

Shalom!

PACKIN'

When young, it was easy to pack for a trip.
Clean undies for each day, a brush and a comb,
Jeans, T-shirts, socks, an extra pair of shoes,
Toothbrush toothpaste. I was ready to roam.

Harder with children: diapers, bottles, formula.
Wipes, water, snacks; a first aid kit.
Clothes, toys, games, crayons, paper.
Song tapes, books and puzzles made a hit.

Now, being old, packing should be a piece of cake.
A road trip, then Alaska land and sea, still weeks away.
Hubby is frantic, so packin' must start now.
I'm not ready, but dutifully start, he won't listen to what I say.

Pills so our blood pressure won't get too high,
Pills to keep his heart from beating too fast or too slow.
Pills so I won't stop at every rest area along the road.
Anti-sniffles and sneezes; pills to help his "flow."

Vitamins, thyroid booster, pills to keep cholesterol down,
Band aids, ointments, for scrapes; pills for seasick ills.
Pills to keep innards moving, pills so they won't go too fast.
Vitamin C to help heal; oops- almost forgot my memory pills.

Antibiotics, just in case, and pills for stomach and other pain.
Don't forget the several creams for bites that always itch.
Cool gel packs, and Biofreeze, for when the sciatica bites.
To keep idle hands busy, my latest project in cross stitch.

That includes many colors of floss in their own plastic case.
Needles, directions, plastic bag, OH! Dull scissors for the plane.
Shaver, pre and after-shave for him; Razors and shave cream for me.
Cell phone, camera, chargers for each, mints, books. I'm nearly insane.

Our deodorants, toothpaste, tooth and proxy brushes, floss, mouth wash.
Night bite guard, container and tablets for the teeth that come out.
Skin lotion, shampoo, conditioner, powder for body and feet.
Nail clippers, finger and toe, emery board – more things to worry about.

Some jewelry, lip gloss, touch of something to smell nice.
My purse that hangs on my hip so hopefully, I won't lose it.
Extra car and house keys are a must. A package of wipes.
In those neglected rest stops, never know when I'll use it.

When we're in the car, pillow for the neck, maps and directions.
Don't forget my sleep pillow. Where I go, it always goes.
Tickets and itinerary for upcoming excursions and cruise.
Okay. I'm ready, what do you mean dear-we have no room for clothes?

"Stepping Into Trouble"

I've always been able to "step into trouble" without even trying. Being an "air head," my mouth is often the culprit. But sometimes, trouble literally jumps on my back.

We had just moved here and Norm had met our neighbor, Hank. I hadn't. We knew he was a Christian by his license plate. The day I threw on old clothes to help Norm put the computer table together in the garage, Hank introduced himself. We exchanged pleasantries and of course, he invited us to church. Heading back to the garage, I commented, "He seems very nice." Norm said, "Yeah, but you probably shouldn't have been wearing that shirt."

"What shirt?" I looked down at what I was wearing. It said, "Co-ed Naked Nursing." I was embarrassed, but later when I took the shirt off, even more so. The back said, "Take all your clothes off, I'll be right in."

Mortified, I called my cousin and told her about it. She was laughing so hard as she said," If I ever come to visit and meet him, I want to wear the same shirt." Horrified, I gasped," Hank already thinks Norm lives in a den of iniquity!"

Shortly after that, Linda, our Bible Study leader, asked if I would help her wrap some of Hank's Christmas presents as they'd done that after his wife passed away.

As I walked past him into the house, I felt him staring at my back. *Good grief! What shirt did I put on today,* I thought. Only later I could take a look. It was a shirt I had received at work for completing a walk for health. On the back, it had the running figure of a woman, sans clothes. OOPS! Stepped into it again.

I didn't often see Hank, but when I did, we usually just said "hi" in passing, from a distance.

One day he stopped me to talk. I saw him staring at my chest. *Good grief! What shirt was I wearing TODAY?* When I could finally check it out, front and center, was a lizard wrapped around a martini glass and it said "coco loco" party time. Things like that happened every so often.

Why didn't he talk to me when I had My "Women of Faith" shirt on? My friend had the answer. "He's over there with binoculars and when he sees a questionable shirt, he makes contact. Of course, that had to be it.

Unfortunately, it doesn't explain the multitude of times I've stepped into trouble in the past as I'm sure I will in the future. My kids are used to it. Norm on the other hand.......

One Pair of Shoes

"Look, Mom," Beth cried excitedly. Those Mizuno running shoes are on sale for half price! That's a fabulous bargain!"

"Are you sure that's the kind you want?" her Mom asked doubtfully.

"Yes! They are the very best! Please."

"Well, since you have your heart set on running that half marathon in September, I'll bow to your superior knowledge this time," her mom laughed.

When they got home Beth couldn't wait to put them on.

"They feel wonderful. I'll just run for a half-hour before dinner. Okay?"

Beth's mom couldn't help but tell her to be careful and not to forget to take along some I.D. The new running-biking-hiking, path seemed safe enough, situated fifty feet off the main road and well lighted along its length of five miles around the perimeter of the park. It wasn't even dark and she'd run it often. No worries.

After twenty minutes Becky's mom heard sirens coming closer. *I hope it's not serious,* she thought. But when forty-five minutes had passed and Becky hadn't returned home, she started worrying.

Suddenly. The doorbell rang. Her heart dropped to the pit of her stomach when the officer sadly said, "Mrs. Arnett, I have terrible news for you."

She was stunned when she heard a car had gone off the road on the curve and had hit Becky from behind as she was running home. No one had seen the accident and the driver had fled. But they would follow every lead.

After the funeral, Becky's running companion, Erin, couldn't stop crying. Mrs. Arnett, trying to console her, added, "Please come by the house tomorrow. I have something for you." She had made a decision and knew what she needed to do.

"Becky would want you to run the race for her," Mrs. Arnett said, when Erin arrived. We had just bought these shoes. I want you to have them along with the new outfit she purchased for the race." She did NOT tell Erin that Becky had been wearing the shoes at the time of her death. Erin's family didn't have much extra money, so hesitantly she agreed.

The next few months Erin trained. The new shoes were wonderful – like her feet had wings on them. She decided to save them for the race and wore her old, heavier shoes for training.

The day came. Erin knew she'd never be first. The Kenyans always won with their impossibly long legs and large strides. But she felt like she was flying along the 13.1 mile course. She came in third with her best time ever.

"For you Becky!" she shouted with happy tears in her eyes.

Two years later when she graduated from high school, Erin had won the ladies division of the half marathon twice. Now as she went off to college, she was determined to win a full marathon, 26.2 miles. She ran as many miles as she could, but it wasn't until after she graduated, that she finally succeeded.

It had been 10 years since she started running. No, she never beat the Kenyans, but she finally won first in her group. That win was for Becky too. Now her life took other paths, only running for exercise and relief of stress. She put the shoes away for a "maybe once again time."

Ten years later as Erin was cleaning out and packing to move, she came across the old shoes. They were still in remarkably good shape for running so many miles. She reluctantly gave them to the Good Will, thinking that someone could still get some use from them.

Thirty-six year old Bella was looking for a comfortable pair of shoes for her fifty-seven year old mother, who had such bad arthritis in her feet she could barely walk. She saw the running shoes and smiled.

Her Mom wouldn't be running anywhere, but maybe they might make her feet feel better.

As Bella put them on her Mother's feet, the crotchety, fifty-seven-year old woman, who looked closer to seventy, almost smiled. *They do feel good,* she thought. Suddenly something flashed behind her eyes. It was gone so quickly she couldn't see it. It happened several more times that day. That night she had a dream – one she hadn't had in twenty years. The young girl running – *what was she doing on the street?* The car swerved. At the impact, she woke up screaming.

"Just a nightmare," she told her startled husband. But the next night, the dream repeated itself. What was going on? On the third day when Bella came to put the shoes on, her mother started yelling. "NO! NO! Those shoes are snarling at me. Get them away from me!"

What was going on? Was her mother having a breakdown? Finally between sobs and many hesitations, her mother told Bella and her husband what had happened twenty years ago.

"Remember when I left you two to go find myself.

How could I forget it? Bella thought. *I was only sixteen.*

"Well I was on my way to this party and lit a cigarette. When I felt a bump and looked up, there was a girl right in front of me on the road. I tried to avoid her, but I hit her anyway. I panicked and took off. What was she doing on the road? It wasn't my fault!"

Her husband's mouth was set in a thin angry line.

"You were off the road on the path when you hit her. She was only sixteen, Bella's age. You were probably drunk!"

The story finally came out. After she drove away, she had gone across the state line and rented a motel. The next morning she called her brother, telling him she was thinking of going back to her family. But when he got there she told him someone banged up her car in the motel parking lot. Three days later, after it was fixed, she drove home and reunited with her family.

Bella and her Dad were stunned. "We need to call the police." He muttered.

His wife screamed, "NO!" But his argument was sound. It had been a long time, she was old and debilitated. Not much would be done to her now, but the family needed closure.

They never learned what made her confess, but she refused to wear those "snarling" shoes. So Bella took them to the Good Will box at the mall for some other needy person.

"Mom, look at this pair of shoes!" Nadine called. "These seem to be in pretty good shape. Mizuno… I'm not sure they even make these any more. But they will be perfect for track running. And they aren't expensive."

"Why those? Here's another pair that looks a bit newer."

"They fit perfectly and they smiled at me," Nadine laughed."

The next three years of high school, those shoes took Nadine to the top. She won the National Track Meet for her school two years running. She was so fast she was awarded a track scholarship for her desired college. By the time she graduated, she won several college national meets, putting her school on the running map. By then, the shoes were wearing too thin to run in anymore.

Nadine decided to have those shoes bronzed, with a photo of herself, receiving a trophy. It was one of her prized possessions.

Years later, she heard her granddaughter laughing in the front room. As she walked in, she saw her, with the picture on the floor and dolls around it. How on earth did that child lift it to the carpet?

"What are you doing dear?" she asked.

"The shoes wanted to play with me." She answered brightly.

"How do you know that?" Nadine asked.

The child answered, "Because they were smiling at me."

SOUNDS OF MEMORY FROM THE '40's AND '50's

SPRING

The welcoming chirp of the first robin of spring...

Large raindrops splatting against the windows...

The gentle, bubbling gurgle of rainwater

pouring into the cistern...

The harsh splashing cascade of water hitting the bricks

when the rain spout was diverted to the outside...

Wind sighing through the budding trees

with a gentle promise of future rustlings...

The cheerful, eager honking of the returning geese

overhead in their perpetual V shape...

SUMMER

An early morning robin, a sparrow, singing cheerfully

outside the bedroom window…

The rapid *chick, chick, chick*, and at times,

the slower erratic *click, click*

of the push mower blades…

The *ring, ring, clang! Ring, thud, clunk!*

Of Dad practicing horseshoes…

The mournful – sounding *coo-coo*

of the unseen mourning doves…

In the long evening, turning into night,

The sleepy, soft *coo-chirp* trill

of the sleepy robins…

The *thunk*! And the echoing tinny rumble

of a can being kicked across the cement

as Kick the Can was the ongoing game…

Then the child's call of "Oli, Oli, Ocean,

All in free!"…

45

At night, crickets – many, many crickets – singing,

violining their joyful nightly serenade...

The roar, then the quickly fading, fading,

sound of trucks that zoomed

along the busy street in front of the house...

Then, the distant, comforting, lonesome *whoo, whooo!*

And the ever –so- faint *clack, clack, clack* of steel wheels on

metal rails from the trains

as they journeyed on their way...

FALL

The nearly silent *shh-shh* as the tree leaves

fall and hit the ground...

The laughter, calls or grumblings

of the children walking to school...

The *scwhhhissssh-crunch* of the multicolored leaves

as they scatter before running, kicking feet...

The seemingly sad, mournful honking

of the geese returning southward...

The hard drops of rain rattling

on the windows...

The crackling of the leaves as they burn

with sweet-smelling smoke...

Scrape, scrape of the spoon cleaning

the pumpkins at Halloween...

WINTER

The heavy, expectant silence when we awake

To an overnight snowfall...

The *crunch, sluff* as we walk on

or through the snow...

The *squeak, groan* of a large snowball

being rolled around the yard...

The *clank, rattle* of tire chains –muffled, sharp as cars travel

on snow-filled or clear patches of street...

Thunk, splat of a snow ball hitting house,

Window, car, tree – or your head...

The *schwish, schwish* of the discarded Christmas

trees as I pull them behind me...

And when the trees had outlived their usefulness

as forts and secret hiding places...

Then came the huge *shwooosh-whoomph* of the

dried trees as they were set afire...

The collective, loud gasping "Ooooohhhh" from

48

the gathered neighborhood kids...

Then the roaring crackle of burning branches, until slowly

the popping and sputtering faded into the night...

Finally, the most comforting sound,

early in the morning...

The *schlaape, schlaape* of the shovel

sliding along the cement floor...

Into the mighty coal bin – biting into the coal

selecting the right lumps for the furnace...

Many years have passed since those memories of sound were made and yet, some of them can still be heard today: The geese, early morning birdsong, wind in the trees, the train sounds and occasionally the ring of horseshoes have not been completely lost. Any gentle waterfall brings the sound of water pouring into the long gone cistern. Some sounds have been replaced. The *chick, chick* of the push mower is now the roar of the power mower. The *clink, rattle* of chains is now the heavy squeak of snow tires.

Now in this high-tech world, there is one sound lost forever- the *schlaape, schlaape* of the coal shovel has been silenced. But when the need arises, I can still hear it. I bring it forth from the recesses of my mind, where the sounds of memory abide.

Re-published From: – "Good Old Days" E-zine

FAMILY

FAMILY

When one excludes all those who have gone before – the long lost descendants – the family in reality begins with Mom and Dad.

Whether society considers them to be a "good" influence, or a "bad" influence, on their children and in their parenting skills, parents are pivotal to the family unit.

Blessed are those who teach their children love and wisdom.

Fortunate are those who also have grandparents in their lives, for there is much to learn as the bits and pieces come together molding us into whom we ultimately become.

My Daughter

My Darling Baby Girl, so dear,
Most precious you are to me.
One of God's dear children so fair,
May I with His help be able to see.

The need of wisdom and understanding,
To care, nourish and guide you aright,
May the links in your life chain be welded,
To ever hold that which is right.

Now you are so tender and frail,
And need a mother's loving care,
I pray that I may never fail,
To do that which is your allotted share.

When to womanhood you have grown,
And life's duties lie before you.
Act well your part and you'll be strong,
To bear the test that's laid upon you.

Someday you may meet the man
Who seeks your love and heart,
Choose wisely as best you can.
Beware of Cupids misaimed dart.

And when you have the vow given,
To the man to be his wife,
May it hold and not be shaken'
With that, which is a false delight.

And if a Mother's place you are to fill,
Accept it as best you can,
Knowing that it is God's will,
For woman to fulfill His divine plan.

And may you in your daily deeds,
Help, strength and wisdom draw,
From Him who knoweth all our needs,
And from His guidance not withdraw.

And when my life's work here is done,
I leave you all in God's loving care,
Trusting that each and everyone,
Will be worthy of the everlasting life to share.

Mother Whitmore, 1941

My Son

My Darling Baby Boy,
So beautiful and fair,
To me there is no greater joy,
Than to give you a mothers' loving care.

God entrusted you to me,
To nourish and rear to be a man,
So may I with his help be able to see,
And His guidance to do the best I can.

Now in my arms, so weak and small,
And helpless in your strength alone,
May the Lord, who loves us all,
Look down and never forsake His own.

I pray that these dear little feet,
Now so tender and soft,
May they walk the way of discreet,
And aim for that which is best to be sought.

And when to manhood you have grown,
Keep step with the progress of time,
Knowing that man is never alone,
But must be ready to fall in line.

Always seek to do that which is right,
And ever shun the wrong,
Then you'll grow into manhood might,
To build a character pure and strong.

54

Someday, a different love than you bear for me,
May come into your life,
As God decreed it so to be,
That man should love and cherish a wife.

And if my life is then yet spared,
My love will not then change,
There is enough to give and share,
With someone else who bears my name.

And if a parent's place you are to fill,
Accept it as best you can,
Knowing it is God's will,
To propagate the race of man.

And when the end of my life is here,
Well glad and satisfied I will be,
To leave it all I here held dear,
For the rest that awaits me in Eternity.

Mother Whitmore, 1941

ON FINDING HAPPINESS
Mom's Decision

My eyes were so crossed at birth and I was such a fussy baby, my Mom sought help. Instead she was given the devastating news that I was blind and would never be able to see.

She would not give up. I was barely two years old when she took me to Dr. Carlin who proved that first doctor wrong. He prescribed a pair of glasses. Fitting them to a tiny toddler must have been quite a challenge. For the first time I could actually see. No more blurry, hazy, smears of life.

That started my continuing appreciation of the never-ending variety of all nature. Critters, scenery, clouds are only a few. There's so much to inspire curiosity, amazement and wonder. As marvelous as that was for me, it only scratched the surface of the lessons life had to teach. We all learn life's lessons, even though as a child we may not see it that way.

Fifty-four years ago on Thanksgiving, my sixteen-year-old brother, Paul, had planned to go duck hunting with his friend, Clayton "KK" Lewis, KK's brother and his brother-in-law.

My mother forbade him to go as he wouldn't be back until after 1:00 p.m. Two uncles were coming for dinner from different areas of the state and we were going to eat at 12:00 noon instead of the usual 3:00 p.m.

Of course, my brother was upset but it was back in the day when parents ruled the household; children did not. He consoled himself later in the day with hunting rabbits and pheasants, and with hanging out with other friends.

The next day we were stunned at the headlines, in the *Joliet Herald News:*

3 HUNTERS DROWN IN KANKAKEE RIVER.

It was KK and his family. They had taken their boat out and it capsized in the choppy water. The treacherous reputation of that river proved itself true in the taking of too many lives. But never before or since have there been three lives taken at once.

I was thirteen and I remember the triple wake. I was stunned and felt numb. At first, I couldn't tell which one was KK. I learned that often when people are prepared for viewing, they may not appear as they are remembered in life

Just recently, my brother asked me to go to the library archives in our home town, to get a copy of that story.

I did as he asked but I was not prepared for the emotional slam when I again saw those headlines. I felt like I had been punched in the stomach; at the same time my heart seemed to be squeezed in a vice. As I fought back tears, I had to remind myself to breathe and kept repeating, "It was fifty-four years ago! Breathe!"

The librarian realized I was having trouble focusing the article on the machine and came over to assist. Being kind and helpful, she ended up doing it all while I wrung my hands in between picking up the copies.

Later, I was asked by several people why I had such a reaction after so long. At first I wasn't sure. Thinking about it gave me the answer. I had learned two things from my brother that I hadn't known before: KK's mother had been widowed for only a few months and his sister was pregnant. In just a matter of moments, his mother had now lost both her sons. His sister had lost not only her brothers but also her husband. Their child would never know the love of its father.

In the intervening years, I too, had to live with, not only the hurt and uncertainty of losing a husband, but also the devastating pain of losing a child. For KK's mother, the agony had to be a thousand fold more than we could ever imagine.

My Mother would be the first to say it was *Divine Intervention*. Had it been a usual Thanksgiving, Paul would have been with them.

I've learned that life is indeed a gift. It started the first time I was given glasses. I could see the world. KK's tragedy slammed it home again at an early age. No one is guaranteed a consistently good existence or specific number of days. The love of family and friends is a true treasure. The joys have become greater, the sorrows and problems have been shared. Strength from God has given comfort, peace and direction.

To behold a glorious sunrise or breathtaking sunset is wealth. Simple things, like the laughter of a child, an unexpected compliment or a smile from friend or stranger, can bring a sense of well being. Birdsong, flowers, mountains, rivers are now largess that is priceless. God's world brings uncounted varieties of enjoyment. So many people never notice the amazing array of everyday beauty.

Our world cannot consist of only mountain tops. There are valleys we must all travel through. Some are very dark and painful. Faith, the love of others and prayer can give us the strength we need to learn from our trials so we become stronger, more appreciative. Without the hard winters, the life renewing spring would not be such a treasure. Look for the sweet nectar in each day. Enjoy and be blessed.

Thanks Dad

It was many years before I realized and appreciated how much my Dad had taught me as a child. He was an honest, hard-working railroad man. He never finished high school because his grandparents needed him to help on the farm. But his hand writing was beautiful and easy to read.

My mother went to work after I was born, because he became ill and was told he'd never work again. He taught me the doctor isn't always right and to persevere. He also taught me when one door closes another will open, and he gave me a strong work ethic.

He taught me to catch a fish with a cane pole, how to ride a bike and to mow the lawn safely. His lessons in life included planting a garden, using tools for minor repairs, how to pump up a bike tire and walk on a roof without falling. He taught me how to like liver because he was able to cook it just right.

He was too young for the First World War and too old for the Second. But he was the most patriotic man I ever knew. Taught me to proudly display the American Flag at appropriate times, and most important of all, he taught me to hold my hand over my heart when a flag went by on parade or the National Anthem was sung. Now, as I look around at so many who do not, I feel sorry they didn't have a Dad like mine.

He taught me to have faith in God and to always do my best. I learned how to care about animals, wild as well as tame, which in time evolved into caring for people.

He also taught me accountability for my actions. When I had done something I had no business doing, the punishment was sure, swift and at times, painful. I never thought he was being "mean." He was doing the best he could to make the consequences fit the crime. And I learned that rights had responsibilities.

Dad gave me the biggest thrill of my life, when I was about ten years old; but, it had nothing to do with me. He belonged to a bowling league and often with my mom at work, I'd go with him rather than stay home alone – we could do that in those days. I was watching when he threw the ball and was greeted with a 7-10 split. All bowlers know it is the most difficult split to pick up.

As he threw the ball the second time, it eased toward the right hand gutter. He walked back with his head down, sure the ball would fall into the gutter. It didn't! As I watched, holding my breath, the ball clung to the edge of the lane. It hit the 10 pin perfectly. As it flew to the left and took out the 7 pin, I jumped up and down, screaming:

"YOU GOT IT!! YOU GOT IT!!"

With a puzzled look on his face, he turned; and when he saw both pins were gone, his whole body lit up with the shocked smile on his face. His team mates were cheering, but I was the loudest.

Years later, I belonged to several bowling leagues. I never picked up a 7-10 split, nor did I ever see anyone else do it. Sometimes the pros on TV did, but they were professionals, after all.

I still smile as I remember that amazing night.

But the most important thing I have him to thank for is not only that he gave me life, but he also saved my life. I was eight years old, coming home from school for lunch as we did back then. I got off the bus and ran across the street. The car skidded seventy-five feet before it hit me. It not only knocked me unconscious but also knocked the breath from my body. My father was working nights and was awakened from a sound sleep. He ran to me, as I was lying curled into a ball, right in front of the house. With no thought about "not moving an injured person," he picked me up. Only then did I start breathing again. I regained consciousness while I was on the couch. I still remember seeing him, unashamed in his blue and white stripped pajamas with tears in his eyes. How does one say, "Thanks, Dad, for saving my life?"

I try, by remembering the honesty, skills, lessons and faith he taught me, as I teach them to my own children and grandchildren. And knowing, the day will come, when I will see him again and will say, "Thanks, Dad, for everything."

MOM'S FAVORITE

Favorite, as defined in the dictionary means – a person or thing (singular) regarded with a special liking or more highly than others.

My kids, especially my daughters, for years have squabbled, in a friendly way, about which one is Mom's favorite.

When Steve was born, not only was he my first child, but he was also the boy his father insisted he had to be. So, of course, he was my favorite.

Four years later, DeeDee was born. While she was my second child, she was also my first daughter. So, of course, she was my favorite.

Nearly six years later, Nikki was born. One might think she had no special place in my heart, as not only was she the third child, but also a second daughter. AH! But she held exactly the same position in the family as I did – third child, second daughter. So, of course, she was my favorite.

Then unexpectedly, eight minutes later, a loong eight minutes, came Erik! Not only was he my last, the baby of the family, (trust me I knew THAT already), but he was the second boy born into a family that for generations had several daughters but only one son to carry on the name. So, of course, he was my favorite.

Now, some people thought, each child was my favorite until another was born. If that were actually the case, then poor Nikki would have been my favorite for only eight minutes – albeit, a loong eight minutes, but that just couldn't be right.

Of course, at a certain moment, I was more proud of one than another. There were other times one was more needy than another. Or one had me more frustrated, puzzled, or fearful. Don't forget that one brought more laughter, joy or peace than another at that moment.

Could my favorite be the one who followed in my footsteps and became a nurse? Or the one who became a teacher of kindergarteners, something I could never do? The one who passed away too young? Or the one who is finally learning to succeed in self reliance.

SO! Who is my favorite? What the dictionary doesn't take into account, is that in a Mother's heart, favorite is NOT singular it's a PLURAL word. They are ALL my favorites!

A LITTLE

BIT

OF

FAITH

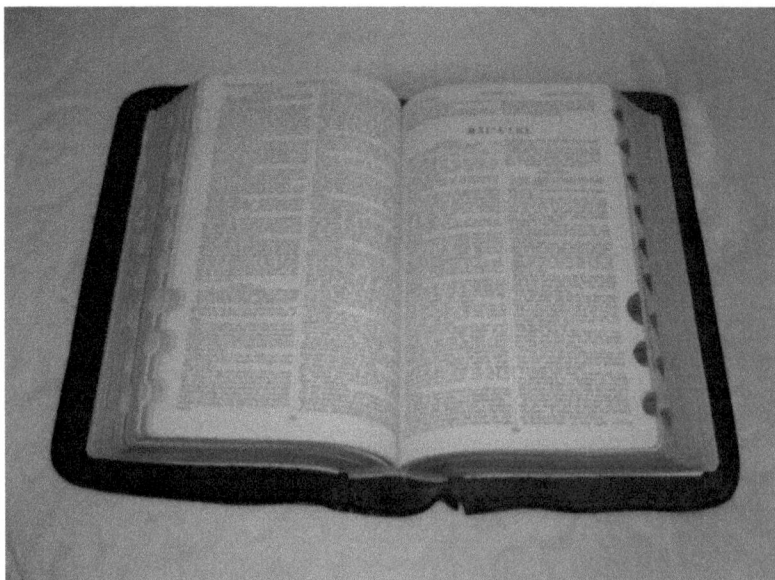

A Little Bit of FAITH

Faith means, "A strong belief, especially without proof."

Or "A complete confidence or trust in someone or something."

Usually it brings to mind religious exposure or training.
To others, that meaning has no part of their lives.

What does "FAITH" mean to you?

The following stories and poems knock on the door that opens into
what faith means to me.

IF

If there was no GOD,
It's a fact there would be,
No sun to warm us,
No air to breathe,
No water running
Clear & free.

There would be no trees,
No Flowers,
No butterflies, no bees.
No animals,
No singing birds,
No creatures of the sea.

If there was no GOD,
It's a fact there would be,
No colors,
No shapes,
No letters,
For us to learn and see.

There would be,
No happiness,
No moments of great joy,
No singing,
No laughter,
No smiles, from any girl or boy.

If there was no GOD
It's a fact there would be,
Nothing
And no one.
Especially no you
And no me.

But there is a wonderful GOD
And that is surely why
We have
All the beauty
In the world,
Under the heavenly sky.

Re-Published from E-zine: *Barefoot on Holy Ground*

GUARDIAN ANGEL

I love caves. The hidden, lurking beauty is just amazing to me. What fun it must have been to discover them.

Walking slowly along, falling back in the group, I suddenly spied something golden shining from the sand. It was half hidden by a rock and looked a lot like a watch band. Oh surely not, I thought, but I couldn't move on. *What if ....?* I slowed to a crawl, gazing up at the colorful stalactites overhead until all had passed me. Swiftly I ran back and before I could have second thoughts, slipped through the rails, bent down to the golden treasure and dug the sand away. It was only part of the rock after all.

My curiosity satisfied, I quickly smoothed the sand and hurriedly headed after the group.

Suddenly I came to a fork. I stopped and listened. Not a sound could be heard. Which way did they go? Which way should I go? "Lord," I breathed, "I'm going to need some help here." I'll go right. It seems to go up a bit.

Meanwhile, in Heaven…."LORD! She's done it again! Is it the end THIS time? Will I bring her back with me?"

"No. It's not time. You'll know when it is."

"But Lord, she NEVER learns!"

"Remember, you took this assignment when she was born. You know the rules. You are with her until it's time."

"Yes Lord, but when she was born she was scrawny and her eyes were so crossed, I knew she'd never see well. I figured she'd stay at home a lot and stick by her Momma's side."

"You did?"

"Yes! Little did I know she would be such a tom-boy!"

"Must have been quite a surprise."

"Yes it was! How could I know she'd climb trees so high where only birds should be?"

"Yes. She wanted to see my world from a bird's point of view. Sweet wasn't it?"

"It was scary! And then when she went to the ball park with her brother, and they used to hop those slow moving freights? That was terrifying. And speaking of her brother, remember when she was five and he was eight, how they used to have to take baths together to conserve water in the summertime?"

"I remember everything."

"Well, I remember that night when he challenged her and said, 'I bet I can hold your head under water.' And what did that girl do? Instead of being meek and mild like she was supposed to be, saying, 'Of course you can. You're bigger than I am.' OH NO! She had to challenge him back saying, 'No you can't!' She almost drowned!"

"You sent Mom in there in time."

"JUST in time! And when she was only eight, she didn't see that speeding car. I couldn't keep it from hitting her!"

"You slowed it down. That was enough."

"But it skidded seventy-five feet before knocking her unconscious and knocking the breath out of her. I had to wake up her Dad who was working nights and send him out there. She didn't start breathing again until he picked her up. So much for not moving an accident victim!"

"Yes, and I told you then. That bonus you gave them by folding her glasses and laying them unbroken on the lawn was a nice touch."

"Yes Lord, but remem…"

"Enough! You've been summoned."

"Yes Lord."

Meanwhile, on Earth…. As I walked along, I thought, *OH, Norm will be SO mad. Wish I didn't have to admit I got lost.*

Suddenly, another fork appeared.

Guess I'll go left this time. I wonder if anyone can actually get lost in a cave anymore? If I could stay down here a couple of weeks, maybe I'd finally lose some weight. Wonder how long it's been? Another fork, now what?

Before I realized it, I was heading to the left.

Meanwhile, in Heaven..."Finally she went the right way! If time meant anything to me, I'd think it had taken an hour! Lord, mission accomplished."

"You did well. Thank you"

"Lord may I speak with you a moment?"

"Of course."

Meanwhile, on Earth... I rounded a curve and the first thing I saw was Norm glaring over his shoulder. He ran quickly back to me and hissed. "Where the hell have you been for the last thirteen minutes?" Only thirteen minutes? Gee it felt like an hour. "Another two minutes and I'd have reported you lost!"

"I'm sorry! I was right behind you all the time. I was just walking slowly." *Bonus! Didn't have to admit being lost.*

Grabbing my hand he hissed, "You never learn! I'm not letting go of you until we're out of here."

"Yes, Dear."

Meanwhile, in Heaven… "Lord I'll stay with her until it's time. But I have a request. Next time, could I have an assignment that's just a bit easier?"

"Such as.?"

"Well for starters, a boy!"

"You think a boy would be easier?"

"Yes! At least they are predictable! You expect them to get into trouble. I will be prepared. And Lord, I don't care if he's a soldier, a trapeze artist or even a dare-devil stunt driver. ANYBODY'S got to be easier than this girl has been."

The Lord's laughter boomed out and rolled across the Heavens.

Meanwhile, on Earth... At last, Sunshine! Suddenly thunder boomed and rolled across the sky. I looked up. Not a cloud in sight. I couldn't help but exclaim, "For Heaven's sake! Where did THAT come from?"

Norm still pulling on my hand said, "I don't know but we're not sticking around long enough for you to try to find out."

"Yes, Dear."

I WANT

I want to see the mountain tops covered with pure white snow.
I want to see the bubbling river in the valley far below.
I want to see the cactus flowers blooming in the desert sand.
I want to see the mile deep canyon, the one they call the Grand.

I want to see the budding leaves in spring and their colors in the fall.
We can see the beauty of this earth because God made them all.
But there is something more I want to do and see.
Something very special that's someday for me.

I want to touch the rings of Saturn and walk on Jupiter's shores.
I want to see the universe, God, the universe that is all yours.
For when in faith we die, our souls to Heaven will surely go.
Then, we'll see all God's glories, we can't imagine here below.

MANGER

As a child, hearing that Jesus was placed in a manger, filled me with peace and longing. I loved animals and thought bedding down in a barn would be more fun than my own bed.

Of course, I grew up and realized the truth of the matter. But still, amid the lights, songs, decorations and gifts, the manger scene was always my favorite.

As kids, we also "believed" in Santa Claus. The birth of Christ and the Jolly Old Elf did not mutually exclude each other.

Until the day my brother yelled at me, "You can't ask for all that stuff! You KNOW Mom and Dad have to pay for everything you get!"

I was heartbroken. No, I DIDN"T know.

So when my own children arrived at the age of questioning, doubting, I explained, "There may be no man in a red suit with a sleigh and reindeer bringing gifts. But the idea of Santa is the loving and giving to others, as God gave us His greatest Gift."

Thankfully, I saw no trauma or anger in their eyes.

A few years later, I obtained a Christmas figurine. It is my favorite. I've been told it is sacrilegious; it doesn't mix; it's wrong." But I don't agree. What is it?

Jesus is lying in the manger. Santa is there. No, he doesn't have a smiling face or a bag of toys. His hat is in his hands, he's on his knees, his eyes are closed in worshipful prayer.

A man larger than life who is loved and adored by many, humbling himself before the Son of God – isn't that the essence of Christmas?

JUST A COINCIDENCE OR...

Life is filled with things we understand and many, many things we do not comprehend. Strange occurrences can't always be explained scientifically, even though some people will insist on concrete justification. Sometimes there are logical reasons. When not, this is often where faith comes in. Others, for lack of a better word, simply call it a coincidence.

But, is it?

My friend's seven year old daughter passed away from Leukemia. Two nights after the funeral, I dreamed about her. I was so glad to see her. As I bent down to her, I asked, "How are you, Terri?"

She smiled as she answered, "I'm burping very well now."

I remembered it clearly when I woke up and I thought *what an odd thing for her to say.*

A day or two later, Terri's Mom and I were talking. Even knowing she was not a spiritual person, I still felt I had to tell her about my weird dream.

I could not describe the look on her face. Fearing I had hurt her, I started to apologize. Instead, she told me something I could not possibly have known.

"Before Terri died she had so much stomach pain, we thought if only she could burp, she'd feel better."

Coincidence? Or...?

After Dad passed away, Mom became too ill to stay in Illinois with my sister, so she came to live with me in Ohio. Being widowed, myself, I worked a lot of nights. But my oldest daughter was fifteen; the twins were nine, and they all assured me they could take care of their

74

Grandma. They did a fine job until she became very ill. She needed her gall bladder removed. She should have had it out years before but the doctor told her then she'd never survive the surgery. Now, there was no choice.

While she came through the surgery well, they had to stop the Coumadin she was taking to prevent blood clots. Unfortunately, that caused her to have a stroke. We could no longer care for her, so she entered a nursing home.

I would stop by every evening before going to work.

On a Thursday, I told her my brother and sister were coming that weekend to see her.

"No," she said.

I thought she was worried about the five hour drive in January.

"Mom," I said, "don't worry. It's not that far and they'll be careful."

"NO!" she said again, stronger,

I tried once more.

"But, Mom, they really want to see you."

Her next, "NO!" was adamant.

OOOOKay! So I gave up.

Then she started reaching for the ceiling toward a corner of the room. Thinking there might be a spider or some other critter she had spied, I looked. Nothing to be seen, just evening shadows. But she kept reaching.

"What do you see Mom?" She just looked at me and reached again grasping with empty fingers.

"Do you see something or someone? Who do you see?"

She answered me with a whole sentence. But her speech was so garbled I couldn't understand a word she spoke. That night the only clear word she had been able to speak was, "NO!"

In the middle of the night, my daughter called me. The nursing home supervisor had called to say that Mom had passed away.

She meant it when she said "NO"! was all I could think of at first. *Now I understand.* I phoned my sister early in the morning. She answered the phone crying. She knew Mom had died.

"Did they call you?" I queried.

"No, Jodee told me."

Jodee was her oldest daughter.

She'd had a vivid dream in the middle of the night. A plethora of angel wings came cascading down. It seemed so real, it woke her up and instantly she knew that Grandma had passed away.

Just a weird coincidence? Or…?

D

The Boy Who Saw Angels

My daughter's first son, Dawson, was twenty-one-months old at the time I was visiting back in Illinois for Christmas. He was such a serious little guy. We taught him to blow kisses when loved ones were going out the door. No smiles or giggles. This mode of saying *good-bye* was serious business to him, as if he had to get it just right.

I was scheduled to fly back to Florida the next day, when I got the sad news that my former mother-in-law, Annabel Parsons, had passed away. I loved that lady! But, I couldn't change my departure time, so I asked my daughter if she would please take my place at the wake.

She did. But, she had to take Dawson and his baby brother, Logan along with her to the wake for Annabel.

My daughter sat in the back of the room with the boys, during the wake, to lessen the possibility of them creating a disturbance – or so she thought. Suddenly, Dawson started giggling. She looked down at him in shock, as she saw him blowing kisses. Then she looked toward the corner where he was sending those kisses and giggles. It was empty!!

People were turning around – some with smiles, while others looked annoyed. Finally, she was able to quiet him down.

When she told me about it, my first thought was that he'd had a *breakthrough* and was now going to give *cheerful kisses.*

Not so! Dawson was now back to his serious demeanor, giving thoughtful, well-thought out kisses.

So then, my next thought was, *Maybe Mom's spirit was there.*

But, no, I believe our soul leaves the Earth very soon after death. Puzzled, I mentioned the situation to Linda Dieckmann, my Bible study teacher.

She smiled and calmly said, "He probably saw angels."

Linda's answer brought tears to my eyes, because I believed she was right. After thinking about it, I decided it made sense. Of course, Dawson wasn't talking at that age, and he was too young to remember it later. Whenever I think about it, I realize how precious that moment was and always will be. It brought great peace to, my heart.

FRIENDS

Friends

Friend is another word that can have different meanings depending on its perception.

There are casual acquaintances, often or seldom seen buddies, fair weather friends, missed or forgotten pals, and the most important, those who are deeply loved blessings. They may be old, new or lifelong.

All add to the essential odds and ends, and to the colorful mosaic of our lives.

Special message to Rose, Rosemarie, Marie and Penny
We have seen more than fifty years of friendship – through thick and thin, laughter and tears, and long distances.

May God Bless all my friends.

Joye O'Keefe
Odds & Ends * Bits & Pieces

A GOD GIVEN FRIEND

When my son, Steve, went to kindergarten, he became fast friends with Andy. He begged to play at Andy's house, but I could not let him go alone. I called his mom, and basically invited ourselves over. That was strange. I'd never done anything like that before or since. Her name was Sue and I liked her the first moment we met. We immediately became friends as her second son was a few months younger than my one year old daughter.

I did not realize then that our friendship was meant to be. Some people said we would have met eventually, but that proved to be not so. Steve and Andy were never again in the same class and in third grade, the boundary changes sent Steve to another school.

We had planned to take the kids to the beach, but my husband forbade us to go. Never happy with our friendship, he decided we were not to remain friends. Why? It was because our husbands worked at the same large company. Mine was in management, and at that time her husband was paid hourly. According to my husband, the two did not mix.

Sue and I discussed this and decided we were not going to give up our friendship. It was one of the best decisions I ever made.

Even after we moved to Ohio, we remained best friends.

I also made friends at church with Ellie and Bruce. While there, Ellie suffered through a bout of breast cancer.

Sue saw me through dealing with Ellie's cancer and a lot more in the next few years, including the death of my husband. Nearly six years later, I remarried and moved back to Illinois, just over two hours away from Sue.

Ellie and I still kept in touch with occasional notes and cards.

One night, when I returned from my bowling league, I had a message that Ellie had called. I went cold. I was sure her cancer had returned. I returned the call immediately, but Ellie could not come to the phone. Her daughter told me Bruce had been killed the night before.

"Killed?" I asked. "Was it an auto accident? What happened?"

A pause.

"He was murdered," she replied.

I was in shock learning that he'd gone to the junk yard with his step-son and the boy's girlfriend. The kids left to get food from McDonalds, and when they returned Bruce was found dead – struck down with a lead pipe. He had died instantly.

I went to the privacy of my bedroom, crying so hard, I couldn't even pray. So I did the one thing I could do; I called Sue.

Sobbing uncontrollably, tears streaming down my face, I told her what happened. In my grief, I yelled, "How could this happen? God says He loves us and cares for us!"

She answered, "He did."

"He did?" I screamed. "How can you say that? Look what happened!"

"He took him home," this dear friend said firmly, as she quietly and gently consoled me.

My sobs ceased as though turned off like a light switch. But the tears still streamed uncontrollably down my cheeks. The litany – *He took him home. He took him home* – played over and over in my head.

I have no memory of the rest of the conversation or even hanging up the phone. During the night, when I would wake, the words hit me even before my memory did. Sometime, deep in the night, I could pray again.

More than twenty years have passed since that traumatic experience. Although, I never really learned the truth of what happened that night, I still keep in touch with Ellie occasionally.

Sue and I still remain best friends. She has helped me through several more very difficult times, including the death of my son Steve. But from that night on, I knew she was a gift from God. That's why, when I found this verse, I cross stitched it for her. The words seemed to fit perfectly.

God never loved me in so sweet a way, 'til He brought thee to me and said, "Behold! A Friend!"

REMEMBERING VALERIE

We met playing Euchre, blonde Valerie with the sparkling blue eyes and stunning smile. Her husband, Frank was a friendly, gentle giant. I liked them instantly. Age was not an issue. I was stepping toward sixty.

Valerie was only fifty years old.

They thought it so funny that I got such a kick out of their last name, "Lane," because it's the first name of my oldest grandson. And then, too, they called her husband "Frankie," just like the famous singer, "Frankie Lane."

I'm not exactly sure when it was that she invited us to their home for dinner the first time, but we had a marvelous time. We reciprocated. We played Euchre. They taught us "Pepper," and we taught them "Wizard."

She was only 51 years old.

Val and I never went shopping or out to lunch. We were both busy but our friendship ran deep and true as we all enjoyed our twice seasonal get-togethers. Laughter flowed freely. There was a time when Val was very worried about the health of her son. My caring prayers continued for months until happily there was an improvement.

She was only 55 years old.

Last April, during dinner at their house, Norm and I made a serious $50.00 bet. They were to remind him this April that he owed me that $50.00. Our laughter rang out in response to Norm's serious frown.

She was only 57 years old.

Last November, we saw Frank in Wal-Mart with a red haired smaller lady. Couldn't see her face, so I ran over to them. Lo and behold, it was Valerie!

I exclaimed, "I saw Frank with this slim beautiful red head and didn't know it was you. I was going to kick his butt!" Our joyous laughter echoed through the store.

We both had been attending "Weight Watchers." The two of us were going to be exceedingly busy over the next few months, so I would call her in March and set up a dinner date – my turn to host.

She was only 58 years old.

Time flew and I was determined to call her on the week end. I had finally succeeded in planning a menu that wouldn't destroy our Weight Watchers' success. In the Friday morning paper, Norm saw where Valerie had been critically injured in an auto accident on Wednesday while driving on Del Webb Boulevard. She was still in critical condition. I could not understand it. She was not a crazy driver. Only later did we learn that she'd had a brain aneurysm – that explained it. No hope remained for her. The family waited until her son arrived then Friday night they allowed her soul to fly free.

Of course I regret I didn't call her sooner. It wouldn't have changed anything except to let her know she was in my thoughts. One must not live in regret. It does not change the past, but it can tarnish the present and it may damage the future.

Still, there is faith and hope that I'll see that dazzling smile again, forever.

"See ya later, Val."

She was still only 58 years old – my friend, Valerie E. Lane.

July 11, 1952 - March 18, 2011

50 YEARS

Of

LOVE

50 YEARS OF LOVE

THE GOLDEN YEARS
Fifty Years of Love

A Golden Wedding Anniversary is a marvelous thing. Sometimes it's difficult to imagine loving and living with someone for half a century.

Years ago the average life expectancy was much shorter than it is now. Many people did not live into their 70s, 80s or 90s, so reaching that 50th celebration was cause for great rejoicing.

In today's world, our life expectancy is longer than ever, but many things have changed. For a variety of reasons, marriage to the same person often does not last for that coveted half century mark.

The following pages contain five short stories of success for that very special, once in a lifetime event.

1. A very talented, undeniably funny, well liked acquaintance.
2. A dear, loved special friend.
3. People very special to me.
4. People most important to my life.
5. Beloved cousin.

50 years of love is an amazing accomplishment.
Congratulations to all who reach that goal.

"CONGRATULATIONS'
JIM AND ROSALIE

It's only a short time since we met,
So your life story I do not know.
But I am aware of something special,
You were married 50 years ago.

You didn't really know what would happen
When you took Rosalie to be your bride.
But you both had great adventures.
Life's been a mixture and quite a ride.

I know nothing of your families,
Your children or those you call a friend.
But your lives have been a blessing
That will continue to the end.

Your devotion to her is apparent
Even after all these years of time.
And her continuing love for you,
Has made the usual, sublime.

So I give sincere congratulations
To you, Jim and Rosalie.
On your 50th Anniversary
And all the years yet to be.

September 17, 1960 – September 17, 2010

Colette and John

There once was a beautiful young lady named Colette.
When John met her, he thought, *I'll just bet*
She'll be the love of my life.

They dated and discovered that, indeed, they were in love.
They couldn't know the blessings they would receive from Above,
They both felt so honored when they became man and wife.

In 1963 a darling daughter was added to the family.
Then '66, '67, '69, boys arrived – until there were three.
What a lovely group, big sister and the "musketeers."

Perhaps they thought their family was now complete.
But '75, a second daughter joined the patter of family feet.
What a houseful of joy, bustle, and problems through the years.

Can't begin to scratch the surface of the multitude of busy days.
Lessons were learned, tears cried, laughter abounded in many ways,
But the love continued to be plentiful and strong.

Colette enjoyed writing and needlework in her "spare" time.
Her poems were amazing, always had the perfect rhyme.
Life was good, but unexpectedly things went terribly wrong.

A roll-over car accident, but Divine Guidance came to light.
A nearly terrible tragedy of loss, but things turned out all right.
That is why this 50th celebration is more special than we can know.

Of course, all who endure are blessed celebrating their 50th year.
But John and Colette hold this privilege especially dear.
Full lives: children, grandchildren, friends and love continue to grow.

Blessings abound and today there shall be no sorrow.
Their theme: *I love you more than yesterday but less than tomorrow.*
Happy 50th Anniversary, Colette and John

August 26, 1961 – August 26, 2011

SHELLEY AND DEE

When Shelley and Dee joined their hearts in love,
They were given Blessings from Above.
Their family and friends cheered with smiles so bright.
They knew, for each other, they were so right.
Because they had Blessings from Above.

Along came the children – Jodee,'57; Kim, '59; Jeff, '60.
Those were the years.
Lovely, beloved gifts from God.
They're all such dears.
Because they had Blessings from Above.

There was much happiness and joy,
Also struggles and even tears.
Sickness, poverty, and riches,
Throughout the intervening years.
But they had Blessings from Above.

Years passed, more happiness and joy
Were given from Heaven
Until the grandchildren
Numbered seven.
Because they had Blessings from Above.

Now they celebrate 50 years
Of faith in God and love.
Because they still have
Blessings from Above.

APRIL 21, 1956 – APRIL 21, 2006

ELIZABETH AND NATHANIEL

They met after she had put herself through Nursing School. Perhaps she was a woman ahead of her time.

He was a hard-working railroad man. "Higher" education was cut short at 9th grade as he had to help his grandparents on the family farm.

The disparity in their educations and "status" made no difference. True love reigned supreme.

Although others called her "Betty", he always called her Elizabeth. She called him Nate.

Three children were eventually born of that union. Their first child – a daughter, was born on December 21, 1935; then a son arrived exactly five years later. A second daughter's birth on August 28, 1943 completed the family structure.

In the beginning, life was not always easy. They met each challenge with strength and faith. Shortly after their first child was born, a house fire caused hard times to come crashing down. All Elizabeth could was do was pray as the food dwindled. They were down to one can of peaches when the doorbell rang.

People from their small neighborhood church, dropped by, making it clear, they didn't wish to offend. But could the family use some of the excess vegetables from their gardens?

With tears in her eyes, Elizabeth gratefully accepted. Needless to say, the results were three-fold. As the congregation continued to help them through that difficult time, they became strong members of that church for the rest of their lives. And for the next thirty plus years, Nathaniel was never without his garden.

Shortly after their third child was born, Nate became so ill, that the doctors said he'd never be able to work again. Elizabeth did the only thing she could do in a time when most women stayed home to care for house and family. She went back to work. Even after Nate was able to return to work, Elizabeth continued at her job, both of them teaching the children the value of a strong work ethic.

That certainly was not the least nor the last problem to be overcome. But in teaching their children faith, responsibility and the importance of perseverance, the family was blessed with love.

The children grew up and had families of their own. Nate and Elizabeth were able to travel while still putting love of the family first.

On their 50th Anniversary, they celebrated with three children, spouses, and nine grandchildren. They were also able to take their dream trip to Hawaii.

They celebrated four more years together. Unfortunately those years were touched with physical illnesses and growing forgetfulness making life, again, difficult. But still, in their declining years, their hearts were filled with joy as they welcomed their first great-grandchild. And their love for each other never wavered.

Eight months after Nate left this earth, Elizabeth followed, to be together forever.

For all those years of love, lessons and hard work, the family was blessed, for Elizabeth and Nathaniel were my Mom and Dad.

April 5, 1932 - April 5, 1982

<<<<◇>>>>

Nathaniel
December 9, 1902 – May 26, 1986

Elizabeth
May 19, 1908 – January 30, 1987

DIANE AND RAY

Developing diabetes at age three, Diane lived a sheltered life. She never climbed to the top of a tree, drove a car or held a job.

At that time, church activities were the backbone of many families, so it was no wonder they met at a young age.

She was attracted to his tall, blond, blue-eyed good looks and the natural kindness that prevailed. Chief among the several things about Diane that touched his heart were her sparkling blue eyes, the gentle sweetness that flowed naturally from her lovely face and her adorable Tennessee-touched accent.

They married when she was seventeen and he was twenty-one, in spite of, or maybe because of the fact Ray had been warned that Diane wouldn't live much past her twenty-first birthday. They took the years that were offered.

The passing years held much sweet happiness, but unexpected tragedies abounded.

Two daughters, Kathryn and RaeAnn, were born to them. Then they wished for a son to make the family complete. In time, a son was born but the grief was devastating as he lived only two days.

Their love and faith gave them the needed strength to continue.

One more child arrived, Lydia. Health-wise she was frail but feisty. Many months passed before she was able to join the family at home.

When Diane's sister-in-law died, they took her brother's young son into their home. Such joy mixed with pain. After only one year, he was taken from their loving care.

94

Family tragedies continued when they discovered that Lydia needed a kidney transplant. There was no way that Diane could even consider becoming a donor due to her illness. RaeAnn came forth in love to donate her kidney to her beloved sister. Sweet success!

In spite of failing eyesight and decreased mobility, Diane's gentle heart remains focused on God and family, as does Rays. His love has never diminished.

Such great love has overcome nearly impossible odds, many pit falls and tragedies through the years. They joyfully celebrated that amazing 50th Anniversary with their beloved children, grandchildren and even two great-grandchildren. Amazing!

Blessings Diane and Ray

September 25, 1961 – September 25, 2011

WRITERS'

BLOC

ASSIGNMENTS

What and Who is Writers' Bloc?

The What....*A club located in Del Webb Spruce Creek, a retirement community in Summerfield, Florida.*
The Who.... *Any person who has an interest in the written word.*

Every person has a story hidden inside their heart or mind. Many do not realize it, do not care, or they think it's unimportant. Others may be too busy to take time to reflect. Some have no desire to share with anyone or they are too shy – uncertain of themselves. That is okay as we are not all alike.

Often, ordinary people will communicate with themselves and others who follow through notes, diaries, poems or memoirs.

Those who come to Writers' Bloc may be the interested ones who have a thirst for learning more or just folks who are curious.

Then there are those who are willing to open their thoughts or experiences to the world. Others have interesting imaginary tales eager to entertain receptive audiences. Many come to the group to better their understanding of the written word. There are those who enjoy sharing their tales of joy, sadness or mystery. Some have been published, others wish to be, and some will, somewhere in the future, reach that goal.

In our group, we have *craft lessons* that teach writing skills beyond those from our school days' learning. We share knowledge that is simple or complex, but always interesting and enlightening.

For some of us the best thing is the "Optional Assignments." We are given an idea, a beginning sentence or a happening for us to turn into a story. The variety of ideas evolving and the creativity of the stories is amazing. One person can make the concept into a story of tragedy while another, using the same idea can bring joy and laughter to the reader.

Here are a few samples I hope you enjoy.

Assignment:

You've been captured by cannibals. How do you try to convince them not to eat you? If that fails, how do you escape?

EEEEEEEK! CANNIBALS!

How on earth could my elephant have gotten lost? The safari had been wonderful. One minute I was soaking in the sounds, sights and smells of the rich jungle around me; the next, my elephant had stopped. My surroundings consisted only of green leaves and spooky sounds.

Can an elephant find his way home? Oh, this jungle is his home. Now what?

Suddenly I saw people creeping through the brush.

Ah! Safe!

Oops, how short lived that thought turned out to be..

In the blink of an eye, scary, painted, savages had me hemmed in. They whisked me off my elephant before I could react. We marched in the direction from which they came. I decided to go with them since they had a tight hold on my arms and vicious, sharp spears at hand.

Coming into camp, the head honcho stood waiting, glaring at me. What did I do to deserve that strange hungry look?

"Does anyone speak English?" I ventured.

A wizened man came forward. His gravelly voice sounded like he said, "Spik a bit."

I couldn't help blurting out, "Who are you guys? What do you want with me?"

Spikabit's grin, with few, blackened teeth was not reassuring as he grumbled, "Dinnah."

They wanted me to eat with them?

He pointed to a large pot where frowning women were building up a fire and a man stood with a sharp knife.

Comprehension dawned!

"I'm the dinner?" I yelled aghast!

Spikabit apparently translated as the unified reply was, "Ya, Ya."

What a crazy way to die. Eaten like a cut up chicken. I said a quick prayer.

"No!" I held out my arthritic hands, yelling, "Tough and yukky!" as I pretended to take a bite of fingers and spit them out. That brought unexpected laughter.

I flopped to the ground pulling off my boots and socks. "Pheeeew!" I yelled holding my nose. They all were laughing now, except the Chief. He never cracked a smile.

Holding out my feet, I yelled, "Bunions, calluses! Yuk! Ack!" Again I feigned chewing and spitting out. The laughter rose, but several were licking their lips.

Desperate now, jumping up, I grabbed my hiney.

"Look! Fat!" Miming tearing off a chunk and chewing, I yelled, "You eat! You die! Heart attack!" as I grabbed my chest, screamed and fell over. The laughter swelled louder. The Chief had his back turned.

Smiling evilly, two men came from the group, grabbed my arms and dragged me toward an opening leading to the steaming pot. I amused them but didn't deter them. Before I could protest, they unexpectedly dropped my arms, melting away as did the rest of the group.

Stunned, I didn't move. Immediately, the forest became animated with a dozen soldiers coming into the campsite.

The first man saw me with shock on his face.

"LIVE! She live!" the solider yelled. They all cheered.

They spoke English to a degree, as they said, "Come outta here," and led me to a small sturdy horse.

After expressing my supreme gratitude, to God and the soldiers, I had to ask, "Why were you surprised I was alive?"

"We nevah fine dem in time. Dey move alla time. No wind, so dogs smell too late. Ha! but no dis day."

'How did you find them today?" I queried.

"Dey alway vera quiet. But dis time we hear da laffing. How you do dat?"

"Oh!" I managed to gasp. "I guess they never had the chance to enjoy a "Dinner-Theater before."

Assignment:

In an airplane bound for New Zealand, a 20-year-old calls his mother and he tells her…

AIRPLANE CALL

"Hi Mom, guess where I am?"

His long suffering mother replies, "How should I know? What are you up to now?"

"Ahh, Mom! UP is the key word. I'm on my way to New Zealand."

"What? You're joking! Where did you get the money for a ticket and why in the hell would you want to go to New Zealand?"

"Check your stash. That's where I got it. You always said I would never amount to anything. Well, I'm going to now."

His mother was livid. What was going on? He had been a problem his whole life, always in trouble of one kind or another. Not like her two younger children.

"How will you become a somebody now? Doing what? You, who's never done a positive thing in your life."

"Ahh – *now* is the key word."

"NOW? What do you mean – *Now*?"

"Turn on the T.V. It'll be on soon."

Just then Mom thought she heard a boom, and the phone went dead. "What in the…?"

Scared now, she turned on the TV. Nothing newsworthy. So she went to the bedroom and checked her stash. Gone! All of it. Anger replaced fear. "That little Bastard," she mumbled.

Unbidden the counseling doctor's words tumbled around in her brain from a few years ago. "Did you drink when you were pregnant?"

"A little I suppose. What's that got to do with anything?" the mother asked, completely burying the fact that she had not only drank alcohol, but had partied a lot – so much so she had no idea who the boy's father was. Even after accepting that she was pregnant, the boy's mother continued drinking until almost time for his birth. Only then did she quit, as she received help from her parents and turned her life around.

But the words of the doctor intruded once again. Looking skeptical he had said "Well, it doesn't take much sometimes. Your child has Fetal Alcohol Syndrome." She barely listened as the doctor explained the symptoms and problems associated with the disorder.

"Not MY fault she mumbled to herself now as she had done then.

Suddenly, on breaking news, "An Internations Airline plane, flight number 2942 just exploded in the sky on its way to New Zealand. More information as it comes in. If you had friends or family on that flight, call this number and leave a number where you can be reached when the passenger list is verified.

Horrified, Mom wondered if that was what her son meant. Couldn't be, could it? She told herself, *even if he had been responsible, all was destroyed. No one would ever know.*

It was big news, and yes, it was verified her son was one of the victims. Friends and neighbors were sympathetic. Until, three days later, a letter came out on the front page of the newspaper. A letter from her son to the Editor mailed the day of the tragedy. He had the nerve to start out by saying, "Because my mother drank a lot when she was pregnant with me, I had Fetal Alcohol Syndrome."

It went on, of course, but she couldn't leave the first sentence. He could not know that. Sudden loud knocking on her door made her jump.

The kids and her husband came running down the stairs yelling. "What's going on?" as they looked out and saw several Newspaper vans and a crowd of people.

Mom fled to her bedroom and locked the door. She went to her closet and brought out the locked box she kept hidden. Upon opening it she saw her locked diary of so long ago. She thought it was so cool to write down her party times and anything else she could remember to be read and giggled over later.

Now she looked in horror at the band that held the lock; sliced clean through. That snot had not only found, but also invaded her dark secret.

The rest of the day and the ones to follow were a continuous nightmare. The lives of her family were in shambles and the tragic deaths of 100 innocent people both caused by her wayward son. Of course she still refused to accept that all of this was the effect of her drinking so long ago.

She started and ended each day, not to mention the multitude of times in between, with the thought, *Boy! I could sure use a drink about now.*

Assignment:

Who or what is the "Apple of your eye?"

The Apple of My Eye

As a young child first hearing the term "apple of my eye," I didn't like it one bit. Having worn glasses from a very young age, I thought it meant someone wanted to throw an apple at my eye. It terrified me.

When I got a bit older, I vaguely learned it was a good thing. As we kids climbed the neighbors' apple tree and spied the best fruit way up high, being so tiny and light, I could go higher than anyone else and pick the "apple of my eye."

The meaning morphed again into a favorite, specially loved person or sometimes, thing. But for me there is a problem with "favorite." It's supposed to mean ONE. I do have a favorite color and even a favorite name. But what's my favorite movie? Well, maybe "Man in the Iron Mask," but gees, the Jurassic Park movies were the "apple of my eye" too.

What's my favorite book? Dean Koontz', "One Door Away from Heaven", might be, but so is the Bible. Also one of the books written by Joy Fielding, among others. It's hard for me to pick just one absolute favorite from among so many.

When I see a sunrise (don't see too many of those) each one is "the apple of my eye" for that day, as are the glorious sunsets. The beautiful flowers, mountains, rivers, deserts and animals. Even some insects are so pretty, they may be the "apple of my eye" for that moment. Yes, even snakes. The albino Diamondback rattler I saw once was "the apple of my eye" for the rest of that day.

And while there are some quite beautiful spiders- you may be happy to note, there the line is drawn. Live and let live, but no spider has been or ever will be the "apple of my eye."

My family, acquaintances, friends, and especially those that are most beloved, each one is the "apple of my eye."

So, I came to the conclusion, the "apple of my eye" is multitude. Why if they were all really apples, I'd have a tree full. No, actually, I'd have an orchard.

Assignment:

Write a story in which:

Emotion...drives...**decision**...drives....**action**...drives....
conflict...drives... **emotion**.

Neighborly Duty

My North side neighbor came into the garage just as I had put the potatoes on to cook. She was talking to Norm so I went to join them.

EMOTION: puzzled, as I heard her say, I don't know if I should call 911 or the non-emergency number."

EMOTION: curiosity. "Why?" I asked. Answer, "I'm not sure but it looks like smoke coming from next door over the garage. (South of me) We went out to look. Was there smoke?

EMOTION: uncertainty. Suddenly, it was obvious it WAS smoke! EMOTION: Alarm!

DECISION: I said, "I'll call 911 if you don't want to." ACTION: I went out back and stood on the picnic table as I dialed 911, and saw more smoke.

The Fire Dept. came quickly. I was thanked for calling them early before it got out of hand.

Three days later, as I came home, I saw my neighbor loading clothes and boxes into her car.

ACTION: I went to her with my arms out and said, "I am so sorry." CONFLICT: She turned to me and screamed, "Sorry? You're SORRY? You're the one who told them we set our own house on fire!"

EMOTION: Stunned.

I blurted out, "Who told you THAT?"

106

She yelled, "The police!"

All I could say was, "I never said that!"

Unhearing or uncaring, she continued. "We didn't do it. It was the refrigerator cord. How dare you make assumptions and tell lies."

EMOTION: still stunned but realized it was pointless to tell her I had NEVER even talked to the police.

EMOTION: anger, surging at her false accusations.

EMOTION: still shocked, angry and now scared.

Oh, I was still sorry. Sorry it happened. Sorry I went to her and trying really hard NOT to be sorry, I called 911.

EMOTION: wonderment. Couldn't help but wonder what a Psychiatrist would make of her reaction. But then,

EMOTION: Realization touched with certainty. Even with my meager psych knowledge, I already knew the truth. Who was it that said, "Me thinketh thou protesteth too much?"

Assignment:

Use the first line of a song as a sentence opening.

GIVE ME A HOME

"Oh, give me a home where the buffalo roam," ran through my head on a daily basis as a child. How I longed to live on a cattle ranch in Texas or Arizona. Before television, it was fueled by the radio program "Bobbie of the B bar B" and the Saturday cowboy movies at the theater.

My mind filled with visions of the desert, mountains, gently mooing cows and especially the horses.

I loved horses. My dad taught me to ride "western style" using my left hand to neck rein a horse, leaving my right hand free as it did the cowboys for use of lasso or gun.

My bike often became my horse as I rode at breakneck speed arriving at my destination in an imagined cloud of dust.

"And the deer and the antelope play."

At age 10, we got our first TV. The cowboy sagas, Roy Rogers, Gene Autry and Gabby Hayes continued to fan the flames of my passion.

During the school year, I was sent to bed before my night owl mind was tired. So it became my habit to picture in my head: me, riding a little grey horse with shining white mane and tail into the hills and desert, finding curious herds of wild critters. My heart would sing. Even the chores were fun and herding the cattle to market was a delight. There was never a problem with choking dust billowing from the great herd of obedient cattle. Nor was there such a thing as saddle sores.

"Where seldom is heard a discouraging word,"

I brought forth a beloved half-breed Indian friend who never told me I was "just a girl," or "too small to be of any use." No, he encouraged and taught me how to rope and brand a calf, shoe a horse, or track animals from rabbits to coyotes and mountain lions. Sometimes, we even tracked rustlers and took turns rescuing each other from a multitude of dangers.

"And the skies are not cloudy all day."

In real life I did get to live in Arizona for a couple of years. Not on a ranch, but that was as close as I was going to get. The real desert was so beautiful. It amazed me that you could plan an outing weeks in advance and on that day the weather always cooperated.

October came. I missed the vibrant hues of the turning leaves. In November, I knew winter was settling in up North and became a bit tired with the continuous sunny sameness. I found myself longing for something just a bit different.

It came on the wings of a severe storm. The change was invigorating but never again did I take cloudless blue skies for granted.

Even after all these years, once in awhile, drifting into sleep, I nimbly spring into ageless White Clouds' saddle. My old friend smiles at me as we ride toward the hills for another day of adventure.

Yep! "Home, home on the range."

Assignment:

Write a story about an uninvited guest... His heart was pounding. He was sure he had seen the door knob turn.

PICTURE THIS

The sun glows through a small oblong window high on the wall of a basement scene. It shines upon a small door in the far wall that faces the stairway under the illuminated window.

Other items are out of proportion to the wooden-planked door – a pair of skates hanging on the same back wall, an old fashioned radio tucked under the stairs, what looks like ornaments sitting in a bowl waiting on a table and a rolled carpet, tied with twine perched in the corner of the two walls we see. All these items are huge in comparison to the mysterious opening.

What is it for? Is it painted as a whimsical decoration on an otherwise bare wall – a child's access to enter or return from a garden when they choose? Or perhaps it's the entryway of mischievous elves sneaking in to wreck havoc or do good deeds during the night.

Or has an innocent door become the orifice for a mysterious "Uninvited Guest?"

UNINVITED GUEST

Sleepily, Mica opened his eyes. He knew it was morning because the sunlight was shining across his private door. Even though a prisoner, he always felt safe on his pallet in the basement of the Giant's stronghold.

They had captured him a year ago, and there was no escape. Not even by the door in his chamber. It opened into a garden with impossibly high walls. The dogs patrolling the area were huge of course – except for the puppy, who could at this time still squeeze his way into the basement. But Mica had no fear of them as they'd been taught to find him, not kill him. He and the puppy were actually quite friendly.

He was useful to the giants. He didn't mind dusting the areas that were too small for the hands of the giant housekeepers. He now had learned their language and they found him, at times, to be delightful and entertaining.

Suddenly, there was a scratching at the door. What could be out there? The puppy never came in unless invited and that would soon end as he continued to grow.

"Who's there?" he called. More scratching. Did he see the door knob start to turn? Was someone injured? He couldn't just stand there. He opened the door a crack to peek out. Too late he saw it, as a large rat suddenly hit the door open, knocking him behind it, against the wall.

He held the door in front of him, trembling. There was no escape. His fear was mixed with surprise. He'd never seen rats in the garden because of the dogs.

He held the door tightly but the rat sniffed him out – knew he was there. What a rotten way to die, eaten by a rat of all things. He closed his eyes and then quickly opened them, as he heard a growling snarl and a squeal. The puppy had entered and attacked the rat. Doing what dogs do best, he quickly dispatched the rodent with a fair amount of blood loss.

Mica fled from the room. The dog followed, then laid down so Mica could climb on his back and continued taking him into the garden.

Finally, they had gone far into the back of the garden – a place Mica had never seen before. The pup lay down and Mica slowly climbed down from his perch, wondering why they had come here. Then he saw it, a nearly hidden drain pipe large enough for him to crawl through. Suddenly, he understood – a way out, to freedom and home. He hugged the pup and entered the pipe.

It wasn't long until he saw daylight and branches across the opening. He pushed out, and he was free at last!

He mused about his flight as he carefully made his way towards his mountains and family. He understood why the pup could not have shown him the escape route before; its job was always to find him. But because of that uninvited guest, he realized the giants would think he'd been eaten by the rat.

Hmmm. Maybe the uninvited guest had not been uninvited after all.

Assignment:

What is your most annoying pet peeve?
Develop a Punishment for anyone caught in the act.

PET PEEVE

Anyone who knows me, recognizes where I stand. So, no surprise when you hear my worst pet peeve occurs when people take the name of God in vain.

Few realize it is a grave sin to use the name of the Creator of the Universe in a trivial, idle or pointless way.

Everyone knows saying "G.D." is taking the Lord's Name in vain. Few seem to realize or care that any time you invoke the name of Jesus or God, and you're not talking to or about them, it IS taking His name in a profane way.

Even the popular teenage "O.M.G." is a culprit, because the thought of the actual words go with it.

Most people, if it's brought to their attention, respond with things like, "Who Cares?" Or, "I don't mean anything by it."

God cares. It means disrespect. "Just an expression" or, Just habit – a bad one." "Freedom of speech. You have no right to tell me what I can or can't say." The excuses go on.

Raised as a Baptist, I was told even expressions like "Gee whiz," "Golly," or "Gosh" or "Jeeze Louise" were swearing. Are they? I don't agree on that point because we all need expressions of excitement, surprise, anger or disappointment. No one says "Consarnit," or, "Jumpin' Jehosaphat" or "confound it" any more.

As for punishment – well, I could slide my right forefinger along my left and shout "Shame! Shame!" Or I could waggle and point my right index finger, yelling, "Naughty! Naughty!" Yeh, that would be effective. Or I could try to wash out their mouths with soap. But I'd just be arrested for assault and being on the short side, I'd have to climb up their bodies, like a tree, to reach the desired orifice, thereby adding battery to the charges.

So, what kind of punishment could I devise? None really. That would be left up to a Higher Power. I am SO thankful that's not in MY job description!

Assignment:

If you could ask any person any question you wanted, who would it be and what would you ask them?

INTERVIEW

The death of actor James Whitmore in 2009, reminded me, I had just one question for someone. All I have ever been able to find out about his beginnings was that he was born in upper New York. There never was a mention of his parents.

You see, Whitmore was my maiden name. When James was younger, he resembled my Dad tremendously. Even my pre-teen great nieces remarked, in awe, how much he looked like Great Grandpa Whitmore.

No! No! Don't misunderstand. I know he's not the illegitimate child of my Father. But Dad did have an older brother, a veterinarian, we called Uncle Doc. He did live in upper New York for many years.

Now Uncle Doc and my Dad didn't look alike and had totally different personalities. But you know how family genes can work. My Dad resembled his Grandfather more than any of his brothers did.

I do not know how long Uncle Doc was in upper New York, but he would have been 26 years old when James Whitmore was born.

So you may be thinking as I did at first, that I'd like to ask Uncle Doc if he fathered James Whitmore. Even when he was alive and I was younger and had some vague suspicions, I never could have asked him. I just knew, if I ever did and he actually gave me an answer, he'd just lie anyway.

So, if I could ask, the question would be for James Whitmore, himself – short and simple. "Whoooo's your Daddy?"

Assignment:

Express your feelings on the "Essence of Spring."

WHAT IS THE ESSENCE OF SPRING

Woman's Essence of Spring

There's mild warmth to the air.
Sun gently caresses the skin.
Cloudy skies are becoming fair.
We want to go out, not stay in.

Gentle pattering of the warm spring rain,
I love to watch through the screen.
Signs of life are renewed again.
The brown grass is showing fresh green.

Crocus peeking through the snow – blue, yellow, white.
Songbirds return cheerfully chirping their part.
We will start to hear crickets in the night.
"Spring Fever" for all things, with love in my heart.

The buds are growing on the trees.
The soil in the field is being turned.
There's a remembered smell upon the breeze.
All winter, for this, we have yearned.

Man's Essence of Spring

BASEBALL!

Assignment:

Write a rejection letter to the author of a best seller.

TWILIGHT REJECTION

Dear Ms. Meyer,

Regarding your Twilight series, I am sorry to say, that while the plot has promise, your characters need refining, especially, sixteen-year-old Bella. She is such a ditz! I'll give her, her clumsiness even if taken to the extreme. But, fainting over a drop of blood! Oh, plueeese!

She is so self-centered, it amounts to meanness. She hurts people over and over, especially those who love her the most – and then she whines about it.

Also she falls in love with a vampire, to the extent, she not only wants to spend the rest of her life with him – she wants to spend the next several thousand years with him. Now, every teenage girl will think her first love is THE ONE! No matter what kind of an idiot he is. How many teenagers do you know who have a lasting marriage?

Speaking of the vampire, Edward's body is cold and hard. It's as prickly as hugging a grave stone. His cold lips would be like kissing a refrigerated rock. He's also a control freak!

And poor Jacob, Bella's Indian friend; he and vampires are mortal enemies. His body is so hot Bella would soon smell like finely grilled steak in his presence. Not good since he can become a wolf. Yum!

There's entirely too much sniffing going on. Vampires sniff out people and wolf men. Sniff, sniff. Wolf men sniff out vampires. Sniff. Sniff. Edward's family sniffs out Bella and other beings. Sniff. Sniff.

When Bella turns eighteen, she's no more mature than at sixteen. She does the stupidest things. Who'd want to spend thousands of years with such a ditzy, self-centered whiny klutz with no common sense? Sometimes I just want to slap her silly!

Otherwise, the plot was quite good.

Sincerely,
Joye O'Keefe

Assignment:

Write a Christmas story using the acrostic approach.

JINGLE BELLS

J – Joy, heartfelt seasonal. Joy bringing
I – intensified feelings until the
N – night before Christmas, longest for a child, bringing
G – gifts from those showing happiness and
L – love of family and friends draws us near to the
E – excitement of a child's Christmas Morning.

B – Believe in the reason for
E – everlasting, gracious, God given
L – love of all mankind
L – living in His world,
S – shining through all accepting hearts.

Assisgnment:

Write a scenario for what happens when the crowd stops cheering,

After The Crowd Stopped Cheering

Some folks go their entire life, never hearing the applause or cheers of an audience. Most people don't care as they continue to live the life they have, doing the best they can. Some just dream about it. Others try their best to make their dreams come true. Some succeed, some do not.

But what happens when there is success, either sought for or fallen into? It depends on the person and several reactions come to mind.

There are those who love it so much, like a drug, they revel in it, need it. For the rest of their lives, they seek it, actively, aggressively. Even when they frequently enjoy the lime light and the adoration, it's never enough, always want more, more. Seems to me these people, always searching for the next applause, miss out on the many small joys of life. They tie their self worth to the adulation of others. And when the time comes, months or years later, the applause dies, they die with it – emotionally if not literally.

Then there are those who after the first time, never again shine in the lime light. Some of them live in regret for missed chances, bye-gone days, and in the *IF ONLY* mode. They too often miss the joys, comforts and treasures that life has to offer.

There are those who have had their 5-minutes of fame, are content with it and bring it to light frequently. Such as the small town lady whose E-mail address is PromQueen52. Others simply continue with ordinary lives, keeping fond memories of their short time in the sun.

There are many more varied reactions of course, but the truth is, the applause does end.

So, how will I deal with the fact, at my advanced age, I was applauded by a room full of people?

The applause from the polite audience was expected – but very nice. Better yet, their laughter swelled my heart, as did the smiles, the verbal congratulations and most important, the hugs. It all gave me a strange deep warmth that I'd only touched before when I was able to make my friends, family or co-workers laugh.

Now what kind of future will I step into? I know I will not crave and chase after the more and more – the needful again and again. It's not in me, even if I wasn't so old.

But, this I do know. The glorious moment will live on in my heart. When life tosses its dark side my way, along with prayers that have always gotten me through, I will also have a small shining gem. I made a roomful of people laugh; that will always warm my heart and make me smile.

SHORT

SPOOKY

STORY

SHORT SPOOKY STORY

Erik's Bio

Erik L. Nelson hid behind his sister Nicole for 8 ½ months to become the surprise 4th child of the Nelson family. They were born on July 11, 1976.

As a teenager he knew his Mom and Grandfather enjoyed bowling. So at age 16 the idea for this entertaining story took root. It was possibly fueled by his favorite author Stephen King, as he sleep-dreamed or day-dreamed. Thanks, Erik.

While he did not pursue the writing field as a career, perhaps… Someday a masterpiece may burst from his heart.

The Bowler

ERIK NELSON

Balding, chubby Dave Wickerson, didn't look like much of a star, but he loved bowling and actually was quite good at it. Unfortunately, he couldn't stay away from the alleys. Being in two leagues gave him the excuse to bowl every night. It never occurred to him he was neglecting his wife, Wendy and eight year old twins, Sarah and Bobby.

Dave started bowling when he was eleven years old. By the time he was twenty-five, he was very good, but never good enough to suit himself. He actually won this particular ball in a tournament five years earlier, and Oh! How he loved that ball! In his "free" time he'd polish it over and over again. The deep red color seemed to glow. He in fact had won five thousand dollars in various tournaments, giving him the reason he needed to pamper the ball and practice as much as he liked.

One day, while relaxing in his study, Dave was polishing the prized ball, when someone called out to him.

Wednesday, October 15th. Glancing at the clock, he could never forget the time – 5:47 p.m. He was gloating at the blazing beauty when he heard his name. He turned and said, "Yes?"

"It's me, Dave" the voice answered.

"Who's me?" Dave asked, puzzled. He hadn't heard or seen anyone come into the room.

"Johnny," the strange voice answered.

Dave had affectionately given the ball that name in honor of his Grandfather Jonathon.

As he looked toward the ball, because it seemed that's where the voice was coming from, it continued.

"Don't tell me you forgot my name."

Dave screamed.

"Dave, what's wrong?" his wife yelled as she came rushing into the room.

"That ball just spoke to me!" he answered angrily.

124

Confused, she blurted out, "Are you okay.?"

Is he sick? She wondered, thinking perhaps he needed more rest.

"What do you think? If your bowling ball spoke to you would you be okay?" he shouted.

"Nooooo," she answered, certain he must be ill, she offered to take him to the doctor's.

"No!" Dave spat. I'm just gonna put it away and then I'm going to bed!"

"At six o'clock?" she queried.

"What the hell's wrong with that? I had a hard day and I'm tired."

Maybe he did need a good night's sleep. Surely, he'd be over this weirdness tomorrow.

Around midnight, Dave was still awake. He thought maybe he was mistaken or going crazy, so he went downstairs. He gingerly took the ball out of its case. Then he sat down, holding it nervously on his lap. He wondered if the ball really had spoken to him or had he just imagined it?

"Yes I did," Dave heard. Startled, he dropped the bowling ball, crushing his toe painfully. He screamed and knew he wasn't dreaming.

"You DO talk," Dave sputtered, barely aware of his pain.

"Of course. I want to have a talk with you, so you have to listen."

"I'm all ears."

"Now, you've won a lot of money with me, haven't you?"

"Yeh, I guess," Dave answered. "But what do you want with me?" wondering if maybe he WAS asleep.

"I'm here to help you." Johnny said simply.

"Help me? What do I need help with?"

"You want more money, don't you?"

"Of course," Dave replied. "Who doesn't?"

" Ah! But I can make you rich!"

"How?" Dave asked skeptically.

"You're a good bowler, aren't you?"

"Well, …yeah…I guess." Dave said. "But I've already won a lot of money."

"I'm talking MILLIONS of dollars here, Dave, not just thousands," Johnny said haughtily.

"Just how is that going to happen? I can't bowl now anyway. My toe is smashed, thanks to you. Now I can't even practice."

"So what?" Johnny sneered. "You bowl with your hands, not your toes. If you'd shut up, I'll tell you."

"Okay. How are you going to make me rich?"

"Place bets on your next tournament. If you do well then you'll get on TV. They'll pay you millions. It's big business."

"Listen to me," Dave mumbled. "I must be nuts. I'm talking to my bowling ball," as he noticed the pain in his toe starting to return.

"And you better listen up," Johnny told him. "You and I are going to make millions."

Dave's wife noticed his toe was wrapped as he limped a bit.

She asked him what happened, but he dismissed further discussion saying he just stubbed it and the toe would be fine for the upcoming tournament.

Saturday finally came. Dave had been pampering his ball most of the day. He fancied the shine on it had an evil glow.

He bowled well until finally only he and a former friend were left in the play-off. One more game.

When he stood to bowl, he muttered," Make me rich!" as he sent it spinning down the lane.

STRIKE! Dave jumped up and yelled, "YES!" not even noticing his toe was still sore. His wife and kids cheered. The voice on the intercom announced, "A strike for Dave Wickerson!"

His opponent, Jim Anderson said to Dave as he picked up his ball, "Don't be so cocky. This is just the beginning." His ball zoomed down the lane, scattering the pins, looking like a strike. But one still stood. Jim picked up the spare but he was furious! Slammed his fist down hard and swore, shocking everyone. But, Jim remembered, he had to behave. He'd been told to curb his swearing and anger or he'd be banned from the tournaments. Swallowing his anger with a large swig of beer, Jim held himself in check, barely. Good thing they weren't on TV this time.

Starting out behind didn't help Jim's game or his mood, as Dave seemed to do no wrong. Strike after strike, he rolled.

The night was over. Dave was stunned! His first 300 game ever! Many bowlers bowl their whole lives never getting that coveted prize. Dave found himself believing in the power of the ball. Or, was it just a fluke?

126

Sunday morning, Dave did not go to the usual church service with his family. He used the excuse of his sore toe, so he could take the opportunity to talk to Johnny again.

Picking it up tenderly, as he sat with his foot up, Johnny spoke. "That was a great game last night wasn't it?"

"Amazing!" Dave couldn't stop smiling. "Thanks to you, Saturday I'm going to be on TV."

"I told you I was going to make you rich."

"Yeah," Dave answered. "I'm starting to believe you."

"How's your toe?"

"Still hurts, but I can handle it."

At last! Saturday! The camera crew was ready and Dave was understandably nervous.

"Don't worry," Wendy, smiled. You'll do fine."

"I know," Dave said as he winked at his ball.

But that night was horrible! The strikes just weren't coming – only two the whole first game. To add insult to injury, his toe unexpectedly hit him with a painful twinge and to his horror, he rolled a gutter ball!

That night he angrily paced in his "den", yelling at the ball. "How could you do something like that? I trusted you and you let me down!"

"It was for the best," Johnny assured him.

"For the best?" Dave's voice rose. "What the hell do you mean, for the best?" he snarled.

"Keep your voice down," Johnny warned him."Do you want Wendy to hear you? She'll think you've lost your mind!"

"No," Dave muttered." I just want to know why you let me down."

"I had my reasons," Johnny answered haughtily.

"Oh yeh? Such as?"

"Think about it. If you bowled a perfect game every time, people would get suspicious."

"What would they get suspicious about? That my ball has some kind of power and it's helping me to win?"

"Well… that's what is happening, isn't it?"

Dave muttered petulantly, "You didn't have to make me lose so badly."

Dave joined Wendy as she watched TV on Sunday afternoon.

"I hate that ball," Dave blurted out unexpectedly.

"What," Wendy asked with her mind still on the program.

Dave, surprised he had spoken aloud, corrected himself. "I just mean, I'm mad at myself for screwing up on Saturday."

"No one can be perfect every time. Don't be so hard on yourself."

"Well, at least I've won SOME money."

"Yes you have and more than once." Wendy was doing her best, as wives try to do, to help Dave feel better.

"Hope I improve next week." Dave sighed.

"I do too, Dear," Wendy encouraged him and the twins chimed in, "So do we, Daddy. Yay for Daddy."

Dave had to laugh.

After dinner, Dave suggested they play a game of Yahtzee. The kids were ecstatic. It had been a long time since they all played a game together. That night Dave was the one to tuck the kids into bed, read a short story and hear their prayers. He felt a twinge of guilt as he listened to their sweet voices. How long had it been since he was the one to help them with the bedtime ritual? Months. So many had passed, he couldn't remember the month or the season.

Bobby rubbed his eyes and spoke in a sleepy voice.

"Daddy do this again 'morrow night too."

Before Dave could respond, Sarah retorted.

"Don't ask him to do that. He won't. That BOWLING is too 'portant!"

Suddenly shame washed over him like a cold wave. When had his family ceased to be the most "'portant" thing in his life? He managed to kiss the kids good night as he sadly looked in their beautiful faces. After he told each of them, a litany from his childhood, "Sleep tight. Don't let the bedbugs bite," he heard soft giggles as he left.

Not sleeping well, Dave didn't wake up until 8:00 a.m. Still, plenty of time to get to work by nine, as Wendy and the kids had already left.

A perfect time to talk to that ball, he thought.

Gently picking it up, he patted it as he sat down.

"All right, talk to me," he said cheerfully. But the ball said nothing.

Irritated now, he raised his voice.

"Talk to me!"

The ball remained silent. Beginning to lose his temper, Dave shook the ball as he grimly shouted, "Talk to me!"

No response. The feeling of happiness from the night before was gone leaving only the twinge of guilt and shame. Not a good way to start his day, but work beckoned. Unwillingly, he had to put it away.

Unfortunately, things only got worse. Walking to his desk, he heard a couple of people snicker. Instead of ignoring it and greeting people as usual, he yelled loudly, "Shove it, guys. Not funny."

That was not like Dave and someone just had to keep aggravating the situation.

"My, my," an unknown voice said, "a bit grouchy today, aren't we?"

"Would it have anything to do with the bowling game, Saturday?" Hank, the office rebel rouser asked.

Dave was angry and frustrated. "Listen! I had a rough weekend. The last thing I need is idiots like you giving me a hard time. So just SHUT UP!"

Hank wouldn't give it up. "Well aren't we the happy bow—ah … I mean, camper today?"

That did it! Dave picked up the computer on his desk without thinking and hurled it toward Hank. Of course, Hank ducked, so the computer smashed into the desk behind him. The secretary sitting there was struck by flying shards. Everyone was struck dumb, even big mouth Hank.

It was then the boss walked in shocked at the mess. Because Dave was standing red faced with his fists clenched, Boss man yelled, "Mr.Wickerson, What the hell is going on in here? Mrs. Bryson needs medical attention. Tonya! Get the first aid kit."

"David lost his temper," sneered Hank.

"I'm sorry, Mr. Matthews, "Dave apologized. "I just got a little hyper and lost control for a second."

"A little hyper? Do you KNOW what you have done? NO excuse for the injury and damage you have caused! Do not take your frustration out on my people and equipment! There's NO excuse!"

"I'm sorry, I…." Dave started.

"You're SORRY?" the boss said sarcastically. "No, you're fired! Now clean out your desk and leave.

NOW!"

Defeated, Dave did as he was told. As he left, he glared at Hank with a "if looks could kill" stare. Hank wiped the smirk off his face.

Dave could only go home. He decided it would not be a good idea to tell Wendy what happened. He needed time to think. If Johnny really could make him rich, then losing his job would not matter.

After a mostly silent supper, Dave told Wendy he was going to the bowling alley.

"It's supposed to storm tonight. Maybe you should just stay home and we can have a family night, again."

"When have I ever been afraid of a little rain?" Dave asked not trying to keep the sarcasm out of his voice. "Besides, I need to practice for the next tournament. I need to win," he said, more kindly.

Few people were out that night and Dave practiced for two hours with no hassle. He was pleased as he bowled quite well in spite of the problems earlier. On the way home he put the ball in the passenger seat so he could touch it for future good luck.

"If you want to talk to me, now's the time," Johnny suggested.

It's about time," Dave said sarcastically. "Why wouldn't you talk to me this morning? Things might have been different, if you had."

"Too late for that, now. Listen up. This Saturday is going to be a big one."

"What do you mean?"

"It's going to be big because this is the game that will start making you really rich," Johnny assured him.

"How's that going to work?"

"You place a big bet, using your house as collateral. If you win and you will, there will be enough to pay the mortgage in full."

Johnny didn't mention Dave would lose his home if he lost, and Dave was too pumped to think about that possibility. After all, Johnny said he'd win.

Dave did discuss the bet with his wife that night.

"Are you crazy?" she asked, aghast. "What if you lose?"

"I won't," Dave answered cockily. "I'm a great bowler!"

"You lost last time," Wendy muttered. Dave chose to ignore that remark as he refused to lose his optimism.

Dave practiced the rest of the week and felt secure in his ability to win. He could hardly wait.

Finally a chilly, damp Saturday arrived. The weather did not affect Dave's belief in himself. He had placed one hundred ten grand on the game. Wendy tried to put on a confident face but she was terrified they would lose their home. However, she did not want to be the cause of Dave becoming uncertain, and bowling badly.

Andy Edwards was Dave's opponent this night. He was a very good bowler. He did not anger easily, kept his cool.

It was exciting, back and forth winning, losing, winning again. Very close games. But Dave lost by two pins. He was stunned. Now he realized he had actually lost their home. What had he done?

Wendy was inconsolable. The next day, she called her parents, tearfully telling them what Dave had done. She hung up the phone, turned, and slapped Dave across the face, screaming, "What were you thinking? You lost our home!" Hard to tell who was most surprised. She had never done anything like that, ever.

"Don't worry," Dave said placatingly. "I'll find a way to get it back."

"How? Wendy sneered. "If you're gonna try to bet it back, forget it! No more betting! I'll make it easy for you. The kids and I will just pack up and go to my folks! You won't listen to me so figure it out on your own. We'll be back when you get your head on straight. You need help and I can't give it to you."

"You're right, I guess I do need time to work things out."

With tears in her eyes she kept her word. Fortunately, the twins just thought it was an outing to see the grandparents. It was easier for Wendy to leave than for Dave to stay. He helped pack her car. He kissed them all and the twins said in unison. "We love you, Daddy," as they waved good-by. He wondered if he would ever see them again. Dave had never felt so defeated and lonesome. He had to do something.

He only had a few more nights in the house. That night he lay awake, thinking about destroying that ball. *NO*, he thought. *I can't do it yet. There is still hope in getting my house back. There MUST be!*

Dave fumed and planned all the next day, not getting any concrete ideas that would solve his problems. He did circle several help wanted ads but decided to wait another day to go further than that. He practiced all afternoon but did poorly. Was it his fault as his mind wasn't on the game? Or was the magic gone?

That evening Dave drove up to "Lover's Leap" with his ball, hoping for some answers. Why it was called that Dave didn't know. To his knowledge no one had ever actually leaped. It was simply a place where teen-agers often parked. It was high on a cliff edge and with a view of the city lights. With it being a school night, Dave had the place to himself and his ball.

Dave figured he'd show Johnny the view. Hanging him over the edge Dave threatened, "If you don't talk, I'll drop you. I lost my house, my family and my job all because I listened to you. You promised I would win! I want some answers NOW!"

"I wouldn't drop me if I were you," Johnny warned.

"You're not me! I want answers."

"I am your only hope of you getting your things back."

"Bull!" Dave yelled. "That's no answer! I was doing better without you. I could drop you right now and it won't make any difference. Except, maybe I'll do better if you're not in my life."

"I wouldn't count on it," the ball almost sneered.

"Well what do you know?" Dave said without fully considering the wisdom, or lack of it in his action. He dropped the ball.

Three days later, Dave landed a new job. Now they could be a family again. The tiny apartment Dave found would be okay for awhile. Things were looking up.

The sun had set. Dave called his wife. The sky was darkening with clouds as well the lost sun light.

"Wendy, it's me. I've given up bowling for good. I want you to come back to me. We have another place to live and can make a new start."

"Are you sure you don't need more time?"

"I'm sure. I've made some decisions. I just need your support now, and the kids. We can do this."

Wendy considered his words.

"All right," she said. "We'll head back tomorrow. There's a bad storm coming in tonight anyway."

"Great! I love you guys so much. I'll start my new job when you get back. Give the kids a kiss for me. Love you."

He hung up the phone suddenly realizing he had never told Wendy he had lost his job. Oh, well, it didn't matter. He would be working again. He was optimistic for the first time since he'd lost their home..

The weather forecasters were wrong again. The storm did not hit during the night, but about an hour after Wendy started for home. It didn't seem too bad at first. Wendy was a careful driver; she could do this. The twins were occupied with their toys in the back seat.

Dave was nervous. He knew his wife had to drive 150 miles in the rain. He knew she could do it, but gradually the storm grew worse. The rain came harder and the wind rose.

"We'll be there soon", Wendy assured the children when they became restless. The rain was thick, Wendy had her lights on but it didn't really help her to see in the murky day. There was a gas truck in front of them which made her nervous. She didn't dare pass or pull to the side of the road. Someone might not see them and plow into the car. She stayed behind it at what she thought was a safe distance.

Suddenly, the truck skidded, sliding toward the edge of the road. Wendy took her foot off the gas as the trucker turned his wheel to straighten. Instead, the truck jack-knifed down the highway and flipped over.

Wendy, terrified, slammed on the brakes. The car could gain no traction on the wet, oil slicked pavement. It slid into the truck with full force. For a split second, nothing. Then everything blew!

By 2:30 p.m. Dave was getting worried. The ring of the door bell interrupted his thoughts. Two State Troopers stood in the rain.

"May we come in, Mr. Wickerson?" The older man asked.

133

Shocked, unable to speak Dave stepped back automatically.

"We are sorry to inform you that your wife and children were killed in a collision on highway 5. They couldn't get another word out as Dave screamed, "NOOOOOOOO! You're mistaken. It can't be them!"

But it was! Only after they called Dave's sister and she arrived, did they leave. Beth took all the information as Dave was devastated.

She went to the funeral home with him, giving him more support than he ever thought he would need. The next few days were a living hell as people tried to give comfort. But he could not, would not, be comforted as Dave was the only one who knew it was his fault.

He was finally left alone. After dark, Dave drove up to Lover's Leap. Standing on the edge of the 250 foot drop, Dave moaned. "I love you, Wendy. I love you, Sarah, I love you Bobby. There is nothing for me here anymore. I join you in "Paradise City."

A heartbroken Dave Wickerson jumped.

EPILOGUE

Jim Anderson, Dave's opponent on that first Saturday night, was driving home after loading his sister's old bed into the back of his new Chevy Pick-up truck. When he passed under the cliff below Lover's Leap, he heard a thump as he felt a bump. He pulled over to see what had caused it. There on the mattress, Andy was shocked to see a dully gleaming blue bowling ball.

When he got home he proudly showed it to his wife, "Honestly, Honey, it just seemed to fall from the skies."

She doubted that but... *Aww! LET Jim have his fun,* she thought.

Jim went to the bedroom and laid it on his bed, the better to examine his find. When he turned to get his bowling bag, he heard someone call his name.

Joye O'Keefe
Odds & Ends * Bits & Pieces

www.ingramcontent.com/pod-product-compliance
Lightning Source LLC
Chambersburg PA
CBHW060307050426
42448CB00009B/1758